After the Primitive Christians

The Eighteenth-Century Anglican Eucharist in its Architectural Setting

by Peter Doll

Church Historian, Assistant Curate of Cowley St. John, Oxford

THE ALCUIN CLUB and the GROUP FOR RENEWAL OF WORSHIP (GROW)
The Alcuin Club, which exists to promote the study of Christian liturgy in general and of Anglican liturgy in particular, traditionally published a single volume annually for its members. This ceased in 1986 but resumed in 1992. Similarly, GROW was responsible from 1975 to 1986 for the quarterly 'Grove Liturgical Studies'. Since the beginning of 1987 the two have sponsored a Joint Editorial Board to produce 'Joint Liturgical Studies', of which the present Study is no. 37. There are lists on pages 44-46 in this Study, and further details are available from the address below. Both also produce separate publications.

THE COVER PICTURE
is from the frontispiece to Lancelot Addison, *An Introduction to the Sacrament* (1693)

First Impression June 1997
ISSN 0951-2667
ISBN 1 85174 347 2

GROVE BOOKS LIMITED
RIDLEY HALL RD   CAMBRIDGE   CB3 9HU

CONTENTS

ACKNOWLEDGEMENTS
The Author and Publishers wish to thank the following for permission to reproduce items in their possession: The Principal and Chapter of Pusey House, Oxford: Cover illustration, 1, 2a, 2b, 3a. The Churches Conservation Trust: 4c. The Archbishop of Canterbury and the Trustees of Lambeth Palace Library: 2c. Bodleian Library: 2d, 3b.

I would like to record my thanks for the many people who helped make this publication possible: the late Rev. Professor Peter Hinchcliff, Mr. Richard Sharp, the Rev. Graham Woolfenden, the Rev. Dr. Mark Chapman, and Bishop Colin Buchanan, for reading and commenting constructively on the text; Fr. Kenneth Macnab for his effort in getting prints reproduced; and Dr. Judy Rissik, for the photographs in Ills. 4a and 4b. Finally, I would like to dedicate this to my wife Helen and to our children Emily and Andrew, who have shown amazing tolerance in putting up with my peculiar passion for visiting churches.

1. Introduction

Church buildings of the late seventeenth and early eighteenth centuries are not well understood. Pugin and his Anglican disciples saw the classical buildings of Gibbs, Hawksmoor, and even Wren as essentially pagan; they despised what they saw as the lukewarm spirit of eighteenth century Anglicanism, and even when church fashions escaped the hegemony of the gothic revival, classical churches were too often seen through the lenses of contemporary Roman Catholic practice; Anglican churches were redecorated and used accordingly (as at Wren's Church of St Magnus the Martyr).[1] Since the Second World War, some of Wren's churches which survived have been re-ordered according to the lights of the modern liturgical movement. The most extreme example of this latest trend is the rearrangement of his Church of St Stephen, Walbrook, in the City of London, where a round, central altar by the sculptor Henry Moore has been installed in the midst of seating in the round. At the root of all these attitudes to churches of the late seventeenth and eighteenth centuries is an ignorance of the principles underlying the design of these churches, especially contemporary liturgical and particularly eucharistic theology.

Perhaps the most common notion people have concerning late seventeenth- and eighteenth-century churches is that they were mere 'preaching boxes' with little in the way of Christian symbolism, 'meeting houses' which had only a minimal place for the sacraments, particularly for the infrequently celebrated sacrament of the eucharist.[2] This apprehension is based on the celebrated letter of Christopher Wren on his notions of the 'auditory church':

'The *Romanists*, indeed, may build larger Churches, it is enough if they hear the murmur of the Mass, and see the Elevation of the Host, but ours are to be fitted for Auditories.'[3]

One of the most eminent of eighteenth century architectural historians, John Summerson, has asserted that 'the unsentimental, unretrospective Protestantism of the eighteenth century' and its architects paid no attention to the liturgical requirements of churches; the architects were concerned with the dynamics of space without paying attention to its use.[4] Even as sophisticated a church historian as Edward Norman could argue that Wren's churches were designed primarily to house the preaching of the Word.[5] In the most

---

[1] See P. F. Anson, *Fashions in Church Furnishings 1840–1940* (The Faith Press, London) 1960. See chaps. i and ii on Pugin and the Ecclesiologists, chap. xxx on the Romanizing influence of the Society of SS. Peter & Paul.

[2] For a recent example of the use of this fallacy, see James Stevens Curl, *Georgian Architecture* (David & Charles, Newton Abbot, 1993), pp.110-111, 121.

[3] Cited in G.W.O. Addleshaw and Frederick Etchells, *The Architectural Setting of Anglican Worship. An Inquiry into the arrangements for Public Worship in the Church of England from the Reformation to the present day* (Faber and Faber, London, 1948) (hereafter A&E), p.249

[4] John Summerson, *Georgian London* (Penguin Books, Harmondsworth, 1962) p.97.

[5] Edward Norman, *The House of God: Church Architecture, Style and History* (Thames & Hudson, London, 1990) p.243.

important recent book on Anglican liturgy and architecture, Nigel Yates has suggested that the approach of eighteenth-century church architects was largely pragmatic:
> 'In the most general terms some major architects, such as Inigo Jones and Christopher Wren, James Gibbs and Nicholas Hawksmoor, had designed buildings which, spatially at least, were modelled on the Early Christian basilica. But this architectural principle was not carried through to the liturgical arrangements, which were designed solely to meet practical requirements.'[1]

What precisely Yates means by 'practical' requirements is not at all clear, but plainly he believes they bear no relation to the eucharistically-focused sacramental practice of the early church, the practice which it has been the aim of the modern liturgical movement to revive. Underlying the modern movement is the often-cited principle enunciated by Gregory Dix:
> 'The apostolic and primitive church regarded the eucharist as primarily an *action*, something "done", not something "said"; it had a clear and unhesitating grasp of the fact that this action was *corporate*, the united joint action of the whole church and not of the celebrant only.'[2]

The reappropriation by the Church of England of the eucharist as its central act of worship has involved the architectural expression of this corporate understanding of the eucharist.

The relationship between the English liturgy and architecture in the context of the liturgical movement has been most cogently expressed by Peter Hammond, laying great stress on the chief function of a church being to house the eucharistic assembly: 'The task of the modern architect is not to design a building that *looks like a church*. It is to create a building that *works* as a place for liturgy.'[3] Hammond encourages church people and architects to embody in the construction of new churches (and the reordering of old ones) a biblical understanding of the church and its eucharistic worship as the act of the whole priestly community, 'the holy people of God who are themselves *corpus Christi*.[4] To this end Hammond argued that the church should be arranged after the manner of a Roman basilica such as St Clement; celebration facing the people at a freestanding altar would lessen the distance between priest and people. As William Lockett has pointed out, this concern for the practices of the primitive Church was no mere historic revivalism or attempt to reconstruct the liturgical peculiarities of early Christianity: 'The Liturgical Movement is securing an understanding on the part of the faithful of the meaning of the Holy Eucharist and their due participation in its offering.' It is concerned with doctrine and pastoral teaching, not with rubrics.[5]

---

[1] Nigel Yates, *Buildings, Faith, and Worship. The Liturgical Arrangements of Anglican Churches 1600–1900* (Clarendon Press, Oxford, 1991) p.4. The most complete summary of the architecture of the churches built in this period may be found in Marcus Whiffen, *Stuart and Georgian Churches. The Architecture of the Church of England outside London 1603-1837* (B.T. Batsford, London, 1947). For a sophisticated description of the architectural development of Anglican church building in colonial Virginia, see Dell Upton, *Holy Things and Profane. Anglican Parish Churches in Colonial Virginia* (The MIT Press, Cambridge, Mass., 1986) esp. ch.5.

[2] Gregory Dix, *The Shape of the Liturgy* (Adam & Charles Black, London, 1945) p.15.

[3] Peter Hammond, *Liturgy and Architecture* (Barrie & Rockliff, London, 1960) p.9.

[4] *Ibid.* p.18.

[5] William Lockett, 'A Lesson in Anglican History' in William Lockett, ed. *The Modern Architectural Setting of the Liturgy. Papers read at a Conference held at Liverpool, September, 1962* (S.P.C.K., London, 1962) pp.45–46. For a recent exposition of this position, see Richard Giles, *Re-pitching the Tent. Re-ordering the church building for worship and mission in the new millennium.* (Canterbury Press, Norwich, 1996).

If Wren did indeed design his churches to focus on the primacy of the ministry of the Word, and if indeed, as Yates seems to argue, there is no relation between the eighteenth-century 'basilican' style and the eucharistically-focused sacramental practice of the early church, then it might well be appropriate to rearrange the churches to express the modern church's reappropriation of the early church's emphasis on the eucharist. If this were the case, such rearrangement as that of St Stephen's might be justified.[1] Hammond rightly offers this challenge:

'The classic appeal of the Church of England has been away from itself and its own past to scripture and antiquity: to the Old and New Testaments and to the catholic fathers and ancient bishops. If we are to be loyal to that appeal, we must be prepared to submit our own past—as well as that of other Christians—to the judgment of scripture and antiquity: the seventeenth century no less than the fourteenth.'[2]

But it is the contention of this essay that there was in fact the closest relationship between the eucharistic theology of the early church and that of the eighteenth century and between the liturgical arrangements of each period. A considerable school of seventeenth- and eighteenth-century Anglican theologians actually anticipated the principles of the modern liturgical movement and applied them to the liturgy. This is not to say that eighteenth-century churchmen and architects had their twentieth-century counterparts' detailed historical and archaeological knowledge of the early church. But if the study of early churches was in its infancy, Englishmen were aware of the latest developments. In terms of patristic scholarship, Anglican contributions were second to none; indeed one work crucial to an understanding of eighteenth century church building, Joseph Bingham's *Origines Ecclesiasticae; or the Antiquities of the Christian Church* (10 vols., 1708–22), has never been superseded.[3] Anglican scholarship reflected the conviction that of all Christian churches, the Church of England was the most faithful to the primitive church. As Eamon Duffy has observed,

'The magisterial work of Ussher and Pearson on the Ignatian epistles, of Pearson and Fell on Cyprian, and of Bull on the ante-Nicene fathers, each contributed to a deepening sense of the continuity of the church of England with the catholic church of the first centuries. More and more the appeal to antiquity became the criterion of orthodoxy, and in that antiquity Anglicanism found not merely its origins, but, occasionally and increasingly, a mirror image of itself.'[4]

Furthermore, Anglican interest in the primitive liturgies was keen and discriminating. Anglicans' study particularly of the orthodox liturgies and of the so–called Clementine liturgy of the Eighth Book of the *Apostolic Constitutions* had a critical effect on their

---

[1] See *Ibid.* p.46 for Lockett's argument that the seventeenth century 'overlooked' this theology.

[2] Hammond, *Liturgy and Architecture* p.25.

[3] See F. L. Cross and E. A. Livingstone, eds. *The Oxford Dictionary of the Christian Church*, 'Joseph Bingham'. One modern scholar, Thomas Mathews, praises as the best available Bingham's treatment of preaching in the early liturgy; but Mathews was under the impression that Bingham's account was only 100 years old, not the 250 it actually was! Thomas F. Mathews, *The Early Churches of Constantinople: Architecture and Liturgy* (Pennsylvania State University Press, University Park, Pa., 1971) p.149.

[4] Eamon Duffy, 'Primitive Christianity Revived; Religious Renewal in Augustan England' in Derek Baker, ed. *Studies in Church History* 14 (Blackwell's, Oxford, 1977) pp.287–8. On Anglican patristic scholarship see also Norman Sykes, *From Sheldon to Secker: Aspects of English Church History 1660–1768* (Cambridge University Press, Cambridge, 1959) chap. iv.

interpretation of the communion office of the Book of Common Prayer and bore fruit in the Non-Jurors' liturgies of 1718 and 1734, and in the Scottish liturgy of 1764 and its many descendants.[1] The intention to be faithful to the primitive deposit as they understood it is evident in both eighteenth-century eucharistic theology and church architecture. In some ways the eighteenth century's appropriation of the early church's worship may in fact, whether by design or serendipity, be more faithful to that tradition than the twentieth century's and have much to teach modern worshippers about celebrating contemporary liturgies in old churches. To demonstrate this, I shall compare eighteenth-century eucharistic doctrine and practice with precedents in the early church. The eighteenth-century evidence will be drawn not only from formal works of theology but also from the standard eighteenth-century liturgical commentaries, particularly Charles Wheatly's *Rational Illustration of the Book of Common Prayer.* I shall then look at the architectural setting of the eucharist (chancel, chancel screen, altar, reredos, east window) in late seventeenth- and eighteenth-century provincial and metropolitan churches, including those of Wren, Hawksmoor, and Gibbs.

---

[1] See W. Jardine Grisbrooke, *Anglican Liturgies of the Seventeenth and Eighteenth Centuries.* Alcuin Club Collections No. XL (S.P.C.K., London, 1958) and also Kenneth Stevenson, *Covenant of Grace Renewed. A Vision of the Eucharist in the Seventeenth Century* (Darton, Longman & Todd, London, 1994) *passim.*

Ill. 1
Frontispiece to Charles Wheatly, *A Rational Illustration of the Book of Common Prayer* (1722).

2. The Eucharist in Theology and Action

It is clear that from early on in the church, the design of churches bore a close relation to eucharistic theology. The primitive theology of the eucharist had many strands, but the eighteenth century church identified itself with those which were characterized by eschatological anticipation, belief in Christ's presence in the eucharist, and the communicants' participation in Christ's eternal sacrifice once accomplished on the cross—aspects which have commended themselves to the modern liturgical movement. Louis Bouyer summarizes primitive doctrine in terms that would come to define eighteenth-century eucharistic theology:

'Here at last all the preparatory sacrifices have found their ultimate consummation in the bloodless [*i.e.* unbloody] sacrifices of that Lamb who has been immolated once for all, and remains for ever interceding on our behalf in the immediate presence of the Father in the celestial Holy of holies as our forerunner. And here on earth we partake of his resurrected Body. And we drink the new life of His love by taking part of the cup of blessing, the chalice of His Blood.'[1]

The action of the eucharist is collective, not one done by the priest on behalf of the people. The priest is the centre of the whole body, but always referring the body to a transcendent focus beyond himself: 'the word of the Gospel, the table of the word made flesh and our food, and finally the eternal advent of the Lord of whom he is only the minister'.[2]

The most basic orientation of worship in the early church was towards the east, the place of the rising sun and therefore 'the only fitting symbol of the last appearance of Christ in His parousia, as that Sun of [righteousness] sung of already in the canticle of Zechariah'.[3] The east was symbolic of the eschatological expectation of the early church, and its importance is evident both in literature and archaeological remains. Tertullian recorded that Christians were often mistaken by pagans for sun worshippers: 'the idea has no doubt originated from our being known to turn to the East in prayer' (*Apol.* xvi). Clement of Alexandria affirmed, 'in correspondence with the manner of the sun's rising, prayers are made looking towards the sunrise in the East' (*Strom.* vii.7). The one surviving pre-Constantinian church, at Dura-Europos, has its sanctuary at the east end. Although some have asserted the influence of the Mazdean sun temples, the justification of such an orientation is clear enough in Christian sources. Clement of Alexandria explained, 'The east is an image of the day of birth, and from that point the light which has shone forth at first from the darkness increases, there has also dawned on those involved in darkness a day of the knowledge of truth' (*loc. cit.*). In a similar vein, Chrysostom pointed to Christ as

---

[1] Louis Bouyer, *Liturgy and Architecture* (University of Notre Dame Press, Notre Dame, Ind., 1967) pp.32–33.

[2] *Ibid.* p.36. See also pp.91–93. On the early liturgy and its setting, see also Jungmann, *The Early Liturgy*, pp.39–73; Benedict Steuart, *The Development of Christian Worship. An Outline of Liturgical History* (Longmans, Green, and Co., London, 1953) pp.33–5; Mathews, *The Early Churches of Constantinople*. For a survey of literature on early church building, see Paul Corby Finney, 'Early Christian Architecture: The Beginnings' in *Harvard Theological Review* 81:3 (1988) pp.319–39; also L. Michael White, *Building God's House in the Roman World. Architectural Adaptation among Pagans, Jews, and Christians* (Johns Hopkins University Press, Baltimore, 1990).

[3] Bouyer, *Liturgy and Architecture* p.28.

the 'Dayspring from on high' and the 'Light of the world' (*Homil.in Zach.*vi.12). Basil interpreted the practice of praying towards the east as the soul seeking restoration to Paradise through Christ the second Adam (*de Spir.Sanc.*27) and Hilary as Christians looking for the parousia, since the coming of the Son of Man will be like the 'lightning that comes out of the east and shines even unto the west' (Hilar. *in Psal.* lxvii).[1]

In his analysis of the worship of the early church, Bouyer points particularly to the tradition of the Syrian church as representing the earliest for which we have evidence. Here the bishop and clergy would sit in the midst of the people in the *bema* for the ministry of the Word. The *bema* would encompass a seat at the west end for the presiding cleric, the gospel enthroned in the east, and two lecterns on either side (south for the Gospel and north for other readings). At the end of the service of scripture readings and prayers, all the clergy, taking the offerings of the faithful, would go the the east end, where the congregation would gather around the altar for the eucharistic meal with the celebrant facing east. This procession and the general movement toward the east express the dynamism of Christian celebration toward the eschaton.[2] As it is expressed in the early third century Syrian *Didascalia Apostolorum*, 'It is required that you pray towards the east, as knowing that which is written: *Give ye glory to God, who rideth upon the heaven of heavens toward the east.*'[3]

The altar represents the localized presence of Christ, a presence in the messianic feast here already begun in the eucharistic celebration. As a result, the primary architectural focus in the early churches was upon the altar. As churches grew larger, it became necessary to adapt the pagan custom of building a ciborium over the altar in order that the altar might remain the architectural centre of the building. Davies points out that in some Syrian churches the altar stood at the back of the apse: 'at Zerzita . . . it was placed against the wall into which architraves from the two columns of the ciborium were inserted.' At Brad and a chapel at Kharâb Shems, the altar was so placed in the apse that the priest's facing the congregation at the altar would have been impossible.[4]

The classical Anglican eucharistic doctrine which developed in the seventeenth century looked to the early church for its doctrines of eucharistic presence, consecration, and sacrifice and for the model of its worship.[5] The basis of interpretation of Cranmer's rite of 1552 was not Cranmer's intentions nor even Reformation theology as such. But even as

---

[1] I am indebted for these citations to J.G. Davies, *The Origin and Development of Early Christian Church Architecture* (SCM Press, London, 1952) pp.81–83.

[2] Bouyer, *Liturgy and Architecture* pp.34–35.

[3] R. Hugh Connolly, ed. *Didascalia Apostolorum* (Clarendon Press, Oxford, 1929) pp.119–120. On castward orientation, see also Josef A. Jungmann, *The Early Liturgy to the Time of Gregory the Great* (Darton, Longman, and Todd, London, 1959) pp.135–138; M.J. Moreton, "Εἰς ἀνατολὰς βλέψατε: Orientation as a Liturgical Principle' in *Studia Patristica* xvii, pp.575-90.

[4] Davies, *Early Christian Church Architecture* pp.83–84, 89–90.

[5] For the basis of this discussion of eucharistic doctrine see Byron D. Stuhlman, *Eucharistic Celebration 1789-1979* (Church Hymnal Corporation, New York, 1988), which has an admirably concise discussion of the issues in the first chapter. For a more detailed approach see Darwell Stone, *A History of the Doctrine of the Holy Eucharist* vol. ii (Longmans, Green and Co., London, 1909); C. W. Dugmore, *Eucharistic Doctrine in England from Hooker to Waterland* (S.P.C.K., London, 1942); Edward P. Echlin, S.J.*The Anglican Eucharist in Ecumenical Perspective. Doctrine and Rite from Cranmer to Seabury* (Seabury Press, New York, 1968); and Stevenson, *op.cit.*

the Reformation intended to restore the primitive purity of the church, so the basis of interpretation came to be the theology of the early church. As the eucharistic theologian Daniel Waterland wrote of the Apostolic Fathers, 'Is it at all likely, that such men as they were should not understand the true Scripture doctrine concerning the Sacraments . . . ?'[1] The testimony of the early church came to be seen as a single whole; citing the harmonious testimony of the earliest liturgical texts, the Fathers, and the Councils in favour of the eucharistic oblation, the Nonjuror George Hickes argued,

> 'He that will not submit to such concurrent evidence, may bring into Controversy, not to mention other things received by the Church in all Ages, the Divine Authority of the inspired Writings, Infant-Baptism, Episcopacy, the Lord's Day, and even the Divinity of our Lord, and Saviour Jesus Christ, and so at once blow up the Catholick Faith, and Church . . . .'[2]

Without substantially altering the text of the 1552 rite, the exponents of the developed eucharistic doctrine read into the rite an understanding of the eucharist inconsistent with Cranmer's intentions and much closer to that of the much admired rite of 1549.[3] Stuhlman observes, 'The Church of England began to develop a eucharistic theology which was at variance with, though not in absolute contradiction to, its eucharistic liturgy.'[4] This is not to say that the influence of the Reformation was negligible. In fact, Calvin's doctrine of eucharistic presence and consecration was on the whole reinforced by the Anglicans' reading of the Eastern Fathers and liturgies.

Not only the theology but also the practice of the eighteenth-century church was modelled on primitive precedents. Even if the liturgy of the Book of Common Prayer was not particularly faithful to the primitive models, in interpretation it was intended to be very close indeed. This was true not merely of eucharistic theology in the abstract, but also of that theology applied to liturgical practice as witnessed in various companions to the Prayer Book.[5] It was a commonplace of Anglican devotional and apologetic writing

---

[1] Daniel Waterland, *A Review of the Doctrine of the Eucharist* (1737) (Clarendon Press, Oxford, 1880) 5

[2] George Hickes, *Two Treatises, One of the Christian Priesthood, The Other of the Dignity of the Episcopal Order. First Written, and afterwards Published, to obviate the Erroneous Opinions, Fallacious Reasonings, and Bold and False Accusations, in a late Book, entituled, The Rights of the Christian Church....* (3rd ed. London, 1711), I, pp.145–6.

[3] Samuel Johnson recalled hearing his father say that when he was young in the book trade, 'king Edward the Sixth's first liturgy was much enquired for, and fetched a great price'; but once Thomas Brett published the whole communion office in *A Collection of the Principal Liturgies, Used by the Christian Church in the Celebration of the Holy Eucharist* (London, 1720), the price of the 1549 Prayer Book was reduced 'to that of a common book'. J.C.D. Clark, *Samuel Johnson. Literature, Religion and English Cultural Politics from the Restoration to Romanticism*. (Cambridge University Press, Cambridge, 1994), p.113.

[4] Stuhlman, *Eucharistic Celebration*, p.11.

[5] F. C. Mather has written a ground-breaking account of the standard of worship in the eighteenth century (including information about regional variations in frequency of communion): F.C. Mather, 'Georgian Churchmanship Reconsidered: Some Variations in Anglican Public Worship 1714–1830' in *Journal of Ecclesiastical History* 36 (1985), 2, pp.255–283. For a detailed and very useful account of architectural details, church ornaments, ceremonies, etc., see J. Wickham Legg, *English Church Life from the Restoration to the Tractarian Movement Considered in some of its Neglected or Forgotten Features*. (Longmans, Green and Co., London, 1914).

that the Church of England among all modern churches came closest to the purity of the first ages of the church. This confidence applied equally to the liturgy. In his Restoration manual *A Companion to the Temple*, Thomas Comber claimed that the composers of the Prayer Book culled from the liturgies of St Peter, St Barnabas, St James of Jerusalem, Alexandria (St Mark), 'Clemens' (*Apostolic Constitutions*), St Basil, St Chrysostom, St Ambrose, and the Roman Missal,

'extracting the purer and rejecting the suspicious parts . . . ; and so have completed this model with so exact a judgment and happy success, that it is hard to determine whether they more endeavoured the advancement of devotion or the imitation of pure antiquity. For we may safely affirm that it is more primitive in all its parts, and apt to assist us in worthy receiving than any liturgy now used in the Christian world.'[1]

If today we smile at the naïve confidence of this statement, it is still necessary to realize that faithfulness to the primitive church expresses the true intention and goal of this kind of Anglican churchmanship.

Charles Wheatly in his *Rational Illustration of the Book of Common Prayer*, the 'definitive liturgical commentary' of the age[2], undertook the task of illuminating the harmony between primitive and Anglican practice. The celebrated frontispiece (Ill. 1) of the commentary sets the tone for the whole work: it depicts a celebration of the eucharist with a priest leading the offering of the eucharistic sacrifice with the congregation kneeling devoutly in the chancel, just as Christ the High Priest offers his sacrifice at the heavenly altar in the presence of the holy angels (the scripture citations around Christ's head refer to Heb. 9.11 and other passages which reflect this theology). The plate also illustrates Wheatly's convictions about the purpose of the division of the church into nave and chancel:

'The nave was common to all people, and represented the visible world; the chancel [in this case the raised altar area] was peculiar to priests and sacred persons, and typified heaven: for which reason they always stood at the east end of the church, towards which part of the world they paid a more than ordinary reverence in their worship.'[3]

As the early church (Clemens.Alex. Strom. 1-7) prayed toward the east looking towards the coming of Christ the true Sun of Righteousness (cf. Zech. 3.8 and Lk 1.78), so too did modern Anglicans.[4] The eschatological dimension of the eucharist was clearly recognized; as Bishop Thomas Wilson expresses it, 'It is designed to assure us of the continued protection and mercy of Christ to the Church till he come to judgment.'[5] The encyclopædic patristic

---

[1] Thomas Comber, *A Companion to the Temple; or, a Help to Devotion in the Use of the Common Prayer* (1672–6) (Oxford University Press, Oxford, 1841) III, pp.7–9.

[2] Richard Sharp, 'New Perspectives on the High Church Tradition: historical background 1730–1781' in Geoffrey Rowell, ed. *Tradition Renewed: Oxford Movement Conference Papers* (Darton, Longman & Todd, London, 1986) p.9. For an important study with illuminating material on the relation between Wheatly and John Johnson, see Richard F. Buxton, *Eucharist and Institution Narrative. A Study in the Roman and Anglican Traditions of Consecration of the Eucharist from the Eighth to the Twentieth Centuries.* Alcuin Club Collections No. 58. (Mayhew-McCrimmon, Great Wakering, 1976).

[3] Charles Wheatly, *A Rational Illustration of the Book of Common Prayer of the Church of England* (1722) (Oxford University Press, Oxford, 1846), chap.II, §3, pp.74–75.

[4] *Ibid.*

[5] *A Plain and Affectionate Address to Young Persons previous to their receiving the Lord's Supper,* 8th ed. n.d. p.7.

scholar Joseph Bingham also affirms the significance of praying towards the east, in 'That Christ made his appearance on Earth in the *East*, and there ascended into Heaven, and there will appear again at the last Day.'[1] And Peter King in *An Enquiry into the . . . Primitive Church* adds this moving passage from Justin,

'As the Sun that arises in the East penetrates through the World with its warm and illuminating Rays; So Christ the Sun of Righteousness would arise with more Warmth and Light, and pierce farther than the material Sun, even into the Depths of Men's Hearts and Minds.'[2]

Although Wheatly advocates an eastward orientation for worship, he designates the north end of the altar as the proper position for the celebrating priest. While he appears genuinely to consider this the ancient position, Wheatly is also concerned with discouraging the last vestiges of the Puritan practice of putting the holy table in the midst of the church; one of the most effective ways he could do this was to argue that the rubric which directed the celebrant to stand at the 'north side' of the table meant for him to stand at the north end of the table in the chancel.[3] Nevertheless, there is good evidence that within the Church of England both the north end and the eastward positions were used. Neither was ever declared the norm or the other illegal.[4] In 1549, the eastward position continued to be the standard as in the pre-Reformation church, but the table was ordered in 1552 to be moved into a table-wise position in the chancel or nave. With the table in such a position, the minister's standing at the north side made perfect sense. But when the tables were returned to the east end and turned altar-wise, the rubric was not changed, thus either causing deep confusion or allowing latitude for interpretation, as the case might be.

At the Savoy Conference in 1661 during the discussion of the rubrics of the communion service, the Presbyterian divines suggested that 'the minister turning himself to the people is most convenient throughout the whole ministration', as the rubric commands at the absolution. The bishops, however, made it clear that they favoured the eastward position;

[1] Joseph Bingham, *Origines Ecclesiasticæ; or, the Antiquities of the Christian Church* (1708–1722) Bk.XIII, chap. VIII, Sect.xv, in *Works*, 2v. (Robert Knaplock, London, 1726) I, p.635.

[2] [Peter King] *An Enquiry into the Constitution, Discipline, Unity, & Worship of the Primitive Church, That Flourish'd within the First Three Hundred Years after Christ. . . . By an Impartial Hand.* (Jonathan Robinson, London, 1692). For this and many other citations on prayer toward the East, pp.21–26. King's emphasis (usually associated with high churchmen) on worship towards the East is particularly interesting the context of a work chiefly celebrated for its arguments against the primitive institution of episcopacy.

[3] Wheatly, *Rational Illustration* chap.VI, §§3–4, p.228.

[4] At a time when westward–facing celebrations have become practically an article of faith as the 'natural' position for presiding at the eucharist [see Gilbert Cope, 'Introduction' in Cope, ed. *Making the Building Serve the Liturgy. Studies in the Re–ordering of Churches* (A.R. Mowbray, London, 1962) p.13 and Giles, *Re-pitching the Tent*, chs. 24, 25], it is worth putting the issue in historical perspective. Bouyer, one of the pre-eminent apostles of the modern liturgical movement, has maintained that celebration 'facing the people' was no part of primitive practice but was a sixth century Roman development reflecting the clericalisation of the eucharist under Gregory the Great; even thereafter it remained the practice of almost the whole church for the priest with the congregation to face east to pray. Bouyer, *Liturgy and Architecture*, pp.50–56. Patristic scholarship supports Bouyer's conclusion: see M. J. Moreton, "Εἰς ἀνατολὰς βλεψατε: Orientation as a Liturgical Principle' in *Studia Patristica* xvii, pp.575–90.

they answered that 'When he speaks to them, as in lessons, absolutions, and benedictions, it is convenient that he turn to them', but 'When he speaks for them to God it is fit that they should all turn another way as the ancient church ever did.'[1]

In the face of such disagreements, a general understanding in favour of the north end might seem a reasonable compromise. The reality is that both the eastward and the north end positions continued in use (Ills. 3b, 1).[2] But it may be that for most Anglicans (despite the overwhelming emphasis on worship towards the east), the eastward position had too many associations with Roman practice and the Roman doctrine of the sacrifice of the mass; on the other hand, the Nonjuring liturgist Thomas Brett may be representative in considering the eastward position 'shocking' because it would, when the priest turned to the people, make it necessary for him to turn his back upon the Altar 'while the tremendous gifts were lying upon it'. Brett also urged Wheatly in his *Rational Illustration* to make it clear that those 'who consecrate with their back to the people are wrong'.[3] This Wheatly clearly did not do, even if he presumed the usual use of the north end.

Two principal schools of eucharistic thought are commonly held to have developed. The first and more moderate school, derived from Cranmer, Laud, Taylor, Cudworth, and Waterland, found no 'proper or material sacrifice in the eucharist', rather what Waterland called 'a symbolic feast upon a sacrifice, that is to say, upon the grand sacrifice itself, commemorated under certain symbols'[4]. The second, derived from Andrewes, Mead, Overall, Heylin, and Thorndike and their use of the liturgies of the Eastern Church, was summed up in *The Unbloody Sacrifice* of John Johnson of Cranbrook. 'This second tradition emphasized the continuity of the Eucharist with the material sacrifices of the Old Testament as described in Lev. 24 and Malachi 1.1-10, and contended that Christ was offered in every Eucharist, not hypostatically, as the Tridentine Church of Rome supposed, but representatively and really, "in mystery and effect".'[5] Each school had its influential advocates and popularizers.

While the two schools disagreed on the nature of the sacrifice, each upheld Christ's real presence in the eucharist. Ideas about the 'reality' of presence have tended to be ambiguous

---

[1] Edward Cardwell, *A History of Conferences and other Proceedings connected with the Revision of the Book of Common Prayer; from the Year 1558 to the Year 1690* (Oxford University Press, Oxford, 1840), pp.320, 353.

[2] The best summary of the evidence for the use of both positions may be found in Archbishop Benson's judgment in E.S. Roscoe, ed.*The Bishop of Lincoln's Case. A Report of the Proceedings in the Court of the Archbishop of Canterbury of the Case of Read and others v. the Bishop of Lincoln* (Wm. Clowes & Son, London, 1891) pp.135, 138. Although Temple when Bishop of London strongly contested Benson's interpretation of the evidence, he conceded that the eastward position was formerly and could continue to be used at the consecration. E.G. Sandford, ed. *Memoirs of Archbishop Temple by Seven Friends* 2v. (Macmillan, London, 1906) ii, pp.663-64. See also the evidence of a correspondent in *The Guardian* for the pre-Tractarian use of the eastward position by George Law, Bishop of Chichester in 1814, by Edward Maltby, bishop of Durham in 1842, and for its being 'an old prevailing practice in the north' (*The Guardian*, 16 July 1873, p.923). See also George Harford and Morley Stevenson, eds. *The Prayer Book Dictionary* (London, 1912) pp.299-301, 'Eastward Position'. For further illustrations, see John David Chambers, *Divine Worship in England in the Thirteenth and Fourteenth Centuries Contrasted with and Adapted to that in the Nineteenth* (Basil Montagu Pickering, London, 1877) facing pp.97, 129, 181, 209, 285, 286, 290, 373, 402, 404.

[3] Henry Broxap, *The Later Non-Jurors* (Cambridge University Press, Cambridge, 1924), pp.332–333.

[4] Cited by Sharp, 'New Perspectives', p.11.

[5] *Ibid.* pp.11–12.

because of the different ways in which 'real' may be understood. To early Reformers 'real' was understood in a narrowly philosophical sense. Thus when the Black Rubric was restored and revised in 1662, 'real' was replaced with 'corporal'. But through the influence of Calvin and the Swiss theologians who followed him, real presence came to be understood in the broader sense of 'true' by both Puritan and high Anglican alike. Calvin 'strove earnestly to guard against an expression of eucharistic doctrine which seemed to reduce Christ's presence to a merely subjective reality dependent on the faith of the communicant.'[1] Thus the first part of the homily concerning the sacrament contended,

'Thus much we must be sure to hold, that in the Supper of the Lord there is no vain ceremony, no bare sign, no untrue figure of a thing absent;—but the Communion of the body and blood of the Lord in a marvellous incorporation, which by the operation of the Holy Ghost—is through faith wrought in the souls of the faithful',

who therefore (the catechism maintains) 'verily and indeed take and receive the body and blood of Christ in the Lord's Supper'[2] William Nicholson, the Restoration bishop of Gloucester, argued how this might be in *A Plain but Full Exposition of the Catechism of the Church of England* (1655):

'We believe Christ to be present in the Eucharist Divinely after a special manner, Spiritually in the hearts of communicants, Sacramentally or relatively in the elements. And this presence of his is real . . . , for he is truly and effectually there present, though not corporally, bodily, carnally, locally.'[3]

Real presence was affirmed, but as a mystery the manner of which cannot be precisely defined.

Another way to approach real presence in the eucharist is by the Pauline term *koinonia*, communion or participation. This is the approach particularly of Richard Hooker, who thus interprets the words, 'This is my Body':

'This hallowed food, through the concurrence of divine power, is in verity and in truth unto faithful receivers instrumentally a cause of that mystical participation, whereby, as I make Myself wholly theirs, so I give them in hand an actual possession of all such saving grace as my sacrificed Body can yield, and as their souls do presently need, this is to them and in them My Body.'[4]

This approach has been called 'dynamic or instrumental symbolism' or 'dynamic receptionism' and is fundamentally Calvinistic. It rests upon the tension or balance between real presence and receptionism. As Louis Weil has argued,

'Much is said, but also much is left undefined. The balance in Hooker's definition may easily be overthrown by a greater emphasis on one point or another. The reference to "faithful receivers", for example, can easily become a basis for a receptionist view if it is not held in tension with a belief that the "hallowed food" is "instrumentally a cause" of Christ's presence.'[5]

---

[1] Stuhlman, *Eucharistic Celebration*, p.12.
[2] Both citations in Wheatly, *Rational Illustration*, chap. VI. Sect.xxxi. pp.278–9.– Of the Protestation [the Black Rubric]
[3] Paul Elmer More and Frank Leslie Cross, eds., *Anglicanism. The Thought and Practice of the Church of England, Illustrated from the Religious Literature of the Seventeenth Century* (S.P.C.K., London, 1951) no. 204, pp.470–471.
[4] Richard Hooker, *The Laws of Ecclesiastical Polity* V, lxvii, 12, in *Anglicanism*, no. 199, p.463.
[5] Louis Weil, *Sacraments & Liturgy: The Outward Signs. A Study in Liturgical Mentality* (Basil Blackwell, Oxford, 1983) pp.49-50.

In the second of the traditions, any emphasis on the importance of faithful reception is absent. As opposed to the 'dynamic receptionism' of Hooker, we have 'dynamic virtualism', in that Christ's Body and Blood are deemed to be present not in substance but in 'power' or 'virtue'. John Johnson expresses his theory of eucharistic presence thus:

1. The Body and Blood in the Sacrament are the Bread and Wine.
2. The Body and Blood in the Sacrament, or the consecrated Bread and Wine, are types of the natural Body and Blood of Christ.
3. But they are not such cold and imperfect types as those before and under the Law.
4. Nay, they are the very Body and Blood, though not in substance, yet in spirit, power, and effect.[1]

Although this theory of eucharistic presence is recognizably closely related to that of Calvin, Johnson explicitly relies for his interpretation not on Reformed theology, but 'according to the sentiments of the Christian Church of the first four centuries'.

Given these explanations of eucharistic presence, the question arises how Christ's presence is effected in the sacrament—the doctrine of consecration. Contemporary theologians worried that the logic of the 1552 rite demands the conclusion that the words of Christ spoken by the celebrant consecrate, for there is no epiclesis or invocation of the Spirit in this liturgy.[2] Both Calvin and the Eastern church held that the consecration was effected by the epiclesis; indeed this was Puritan doctrine according to the Westminster Directory, the standard of worship under the Commonwealth.[3] The great patristic scholar Bishop George Bull tried to work around this stumbling block in *The Corruptions of the Church of Rome*, attempting to conform an invocation of the Spirit model to the Prayer Book rite. Citing Justin and Irenaeus, Bull argued:

'By or upon the sacerdotal benediction, the Spirit of Christ, or a divine virtue of Christ descends upon the elements, and accompanies them to all faithful communicants, and . . . therefore they are said to be and are the Body and Blood of Christ; the same divinity which is hypostatically united to the Body of Christ in heaven, being virtually united to the elements of Bread and Wine upon the earth. Which also seems to be the meaning of all the ancient liturgies, in which it is prayed, "that God would send down His Spirit upon the bread and wine in the Eucharist".'[4]

---

[1] (Johnson's title is worth citing in full as a summary of his eucharistic theology.) *The Unbloody Sacrifice, and Altar, Unvailed and Supported, in which the nature of the Eucharist is explained according to the sentiments of the Christian Church in the first four centuries; Proving, That the Eucharist is a proper material Sacrifice, That it is both Eucharistic and propitiatory, That it is to be offered by proper officers, That the Oblation is to be made on a proper Altar, That it is properly consumed by manducation . . .* (1704) Library of Anglo–Catholic Theology (John Henry Parker, Oxford, 1847) pp.321–322. Grisbrooke wonders (p.71) how Johnson reconciled this teaching with the liturgy of 1662. Wheatly and Hickes (see below) may offer answers for this, however unsatisfactory.

[2] Cranmer himself wanted to avoid any indication of a 'moment' of consecration. See Colin Buchanan, *What did Cranmer think he was doing?* (Grove Liturgical Study 7, Bramcote, 1976) pp.23-25; cf. Diarmaid McCulloch, *Thomas Cranmer* (Yale University Press, New Haven, 1996) p.502.

[3] Stuhlman, *Eucharistic Celebration*, p.17. Stuhlman claims this to be the 'more usual' interpretation, but it is absent from such standard divines as Waterland (see below).

[4] Cited in Stone, *A History* ii, p.448.

Waterland also tries to remain faithful to the Prayer Book rite but to avoid a 'Romanist' interpretation. Based on his reading of Chrysostom, he argues that 'This is my Body' 'is not meant (as the Romanists are pleased to interpret) that the pronouncing these words makes the consecration: but the words then spoken by our blessed Lord are conceived to operate now as *virtually* [my emphasis] carrying in them a rule, or a promise, for all succeeding ages of the Church, that what was then done when our Lord himself administered, or consecrated, will always be done in the celebration of the eucharist,pursuant to that original. . . . What the Sacrament then was, in meaning, virtue, and effect, the same it is also at this day. . . . The same Lord is our High Priest in heaven, recommending and enforcing our prayer there, and still constantly ratifying what he once said, "This is my Body", &c.'[1]

It is telling to see 'virtualism' crop up here in a 'dynamic receptionist' interpretation.

Interestingly, in the case of consecration, Johnson does not wholly endorse the Eastern approach; he affirms that the Holy Ghost was 'by vote of antiquity, the principal immediate cause' of bread and wine becoming Body and Blood, but he added three 'subordinate or mediate' causes: 1. The reciting the words of institution; 2. The oblation of the symbols; and 3. The prayer of invocation. He argues that in the ancient liturgies these causes followed one another in order and were all held to contribute to the consecration. Therefore Johnson argues that the theology of consecration of the early Church is distinct from both the Roman and Greek approaches: 'The Church of Rome attributes the consecration wholly to the words of institution; the Greek Church wholly to the prayer of invocation; but I conceive the ancients did not attribute the consecration to any one of these actions in such a manner as to exclude the other.'[2] Because of the importance to them of the epiclesis upon the elements, Johnson and others of his tradition preferred to 1549 and 1637 rites to those of 1552 and 1662; Johnson's liturgical thinking was central to the liturgies of the Nonjurors (who put his theories into practice) and thus to the Scottish rite of 1764 and the various Anglican liturgies (particularly of the American Episcopal Church) descended from it.[3]

Waterland strongly criticized Johnson's ideas about the function of the Holy Ghost in the eucharist, regarding the 'union of the Spirit with the elements (rather than with the persons)' as a 'gross notion, and groundless'.[4] Waterland believed the action of the Spirit could not make the elements into the Body and Blood; as Dugmore expresses it, 'the notion would resolve itself into a kind of impanation of the Spirit.'[5] Johnson's theory would make Christ's body available to both worthy and unworthy recipients; therefore Waterland clung to a Hookerian notion of worthy reception.

The commentators unanimously warned against the danger of interpreting the consecration as effected by the words of institution and argued for the role of the Holy Ghost and/or of the prayer of the whole church. Wheatly in particular strains his argument

---

[1] Waterland, *A Review*, p.87. His citation of Chysostom is to the Homil. i. de Proditione Judae.
[2] Johnson, *The Unbloody Sacrifice*, pp.329–330, 331.
[3] Grisbrooke, *Anglican Liturgies*, p.71.
[4] Waterland, *A Review*, pp.82–83.
[5] Dugmore, *Eucharistic Doctrine*, p.179.

to the utmost to conjure up an epiclesis upon the elements in the 1662 rite:
'There was always inserted in the primitive forms a particular petition for the descent of the Holy Ghost upon the Sacramental Elements, which was also continued in the first liturgy of King Edw.VI. in very express and open terms . . . [with thy holy Spirite & Word, vouchsafe to bl+esse and sanc+tifie these thy gifts . . .]. This upon the scruples of Bucer, (whom I am sorry I have so often occasion to name,) was left out at the review in the fifth of king Edward; and the following sentence, which he was pleased to allow of, inserted in its stead [grant that we receiving thy creatures . . .]. In these words, it is true, the sense of the former is still implied, and consequently by these the elements are now consecrated, and so become the body and blood of our Saviour Christ.'[1]
The implication is that the consecration is by the Spirit, whether expressly invoked upon the elements or not.

George Hickes strives to obviate the implicit consecration by the words of institution in a different way, pointing to the two oblations of the elements in the ancient eucharist, the one preceding and the other coming after the consecration (citing Justin *Apol* I, §86,*Const. Apol. Lib.* VIII cap. 12, and St Cyril of Jerusalem *Catechis. Mystag.* V, §§IV, V, VI). He then observes,

'In our present Liturgy, the first Oblation is made in the beginning of the Prayer for the whole State of Christ's Church, immediately after the Priest hath placed the Bread, and Wine upon the Table, in these Words, *Almighty and Everlasting God — we humbly beseech thee to accept our Alms and Oblations.* And the latter is made in substance, and according to the intention of the Church in the Prayer of Consecration to God the Father, where after the Commemoration of Christ's offering himself upon the Cross, and his institution of the perpetual Memorial of his precious Death, God the Father is implor'd to hear us, while, *according to the same Institution, we receive his Creatures of Bread and Wine, in remembrance of his* Son our *Saviour's* Death and *Passion....*'[2]

In William Nicholls'*A Comment on the Book of Common Prayer* (1720), there is no discussion of the role of the Spirit; he recites the epiclesis on the elements from the 1549 rite without comment save that the source was the Liturgy of St John Chrysostom. To avoid the 'Romanist' trap of consecration by the words of institution, he affirms the position of the early church that the elements were consecrated with the prayer of the church. In a typical passage of Anglican patristic exegesis Nicholls writes,

'For, as for Prayer, That the Elements were consecrated with it, and not only by the bare repeating of the Institution Words, we have the Testimony of *Justin Martyr,* who says, that the *Bread was eucarisqbnai dia euchV, made the Sacrament or Eucharist by Prayer.* Just.Mart. Ap.II. And also of *Origen, prosagomenouV artouV esqiomen swma genomenouV dia thn euchn. We eat the Bread which is offered, being made a Body by Prayer.* Orig.Cont.Cel. Lib.8. And St Ambrose, *Quotiscunque Sacramenta sumimus, quae per* Sacrae Orationis *mysterium in carnem transfigurantur.* When we eat the Sacrament, which by the Mystery of Prayer is transfigured into Christ's Body. *Amb.de fide* . . . . Which Passages, and many other in ancient Writers of the like kind, shew, that the Real Presence of Christ's Body and Blood was owing chiefly to the Prayer of the Church.'[3]

---

[1] Wheatly, *Rational Illustration* Chap.VI, Sect. xxii, §2, pp.254–255.
[2] Hickes, *Two Treatises* I, pp.118–120.
[3] William Nicholls, *A Comment on the Book of Common Prayer* . . . (London, 1720), n.p. The Communion [of the Consecration]

The consecration is thus the corporate act of the whole community of the faithful, not the result of the words of the priest; this central tenet of the modern liturgical movement was clearly understood in the early eighteenth century. Nicholls does however argue that the recitation of the words of institution was primitive practice; this 'is clear from the Apostolical Constitutions, Lib.VIII,cap.12, where not only the Words of the Institution, but the Consecration Prayer is expressed almost exactly as ours is.'[1] But he is anxious to refute any suggestion that the recitations of the words of institution made the consecration. Wheatly further demonstrates the need for such insistence by pointing out that the rubric for the consecration of further elements reinforces the impression that consecration is made by the words of institution, for it is these that are to be recited.[2]

Closely related to consecration is the doctrine of eucharistic sacrifice. Anglican theologians' objections to the mediæval doctrine as they understood it are expressed in Article XXXI:

> 'The Offering of Christ once made is that perfect redemption, propitiation, and satisfaction, for all the sins of the whole world, both original and actual; and there is none other satisfaction for sin, but that alone, Wherefore the sacrifice of Masses, in which it was commonly said, that the Priest did offer Christ for the quick and the dead, to have remission of pain or guilt, were blasphemous fables, and dangerous deceits.'

The reformers wanted to avoid any notion of an independent sacrifice in each eucharistic oblation, an idea arising from the Roman canon's offering of the bread and wine to God *after* the institution narrative (i.e. after its consecration into the Body and Blood).

Cranmer's prayer of oblation after communion uses sacrifice three times—'sacrifice of praise and thanksgiving', 'holy and living sacrifice', and 'unworthy to offer thee any sacrifice'. Thus the rite avoided any suggestion of the bread and wine being offered in the eucharist. But could such a sacrifice as it was have any efficacy without supplanting the effect of Christ's sacrifice? Bramhall stated a positive doctrine of sacrifice of every sort short of a suppletory sacrifice (having its own efficacy apart from the Cross), asserting a 'Sacrifice of praise and thanksgiving', a 'Commemorative sacrifice', a 'representative sacrifice', 'an impetrative sacrifice', and 'an applicative sacrifice', all in some way dependent on the one sacrifice on the Cross.[3] Bramhall's contemporary Jeremy Taylor used the Christology of Hebrews 9 and 10 to describe Christ as high priest after the order of Melchizedek pleading his sacrifice in the heavenly sanctuary even as the priest pleads it in the church's eucharist.[4] Thus,

> 'The church being the image of heaven, the priest the minister of Christ; the holy table being the copy of the celestial altar, and the eternal sacrifice of the lamb slain from the beginning of the world being always the same; it bleeds no more after the finishing of it on the cross, but it is wonderfully represented in heaven, and graciously represented here; by Christ's action there, by his commandment here.'[5]

The eucharistic doctrine implicit in the frontispiece to Wheatly's *Rational Illustration* is thus given full theological expression.

---

[1] *Ibid.*

[2] Wheatly, *Rational Illustration* ch.VI, Sect.xxii, 2.

[3] *Anglicanism*, no. 214, p.496.

[4] Although Grisbrooke, *Anglican Liturgies* p.27, argues that Taylor was the first Anglican to articulate this theology, William Forbes does the same; see *Anglicanism* no.205, pp.471–473. On Forbes see Stevenson, *Covenant* pp.77–83.

[5] Jeremy Taylor, *The Worthy Communicant* (1660), cited in Dugmore, *Eucharistic Doctrine* p.102.

The question of whether the priest offers a material sacrifice depends on one's interpretation of how the bread and wine are used. Those arguing for a material sacrifice followed Symon Patrick in interpreting the restoration of the word 'oblation' in the prayer for the church militant and of the rubric for 'placing' the bread and wine on the altar in the 1662 rite as indicating an oblation of thanksgiving to God for the fruits of the earth. For Patrick, this oblation was distinct from the 'alms' of money; the oblations 'can signify nothing else but (according to the style of the ancient Church) this bread and wine presented to God in a thankful remembrance of our food both dry and liquid (as Justin Martyr speaks), which he, the Creator of the world, hath made and given to us.'[1]

For Johnson, the oblation of the bread and wine is the offering of the 'authoritative representations of Christ's Body and Blood'; the bread and wine are that 'upon which God, at the prayers of the Priests and people, sends down His peculiar spiritual benediction, by which it becomes a Sacrifice of a sweet-smelling savour, as being therefore fully consecrated into the spiritual Body and Blood of Christ, and therefore fit with which to propitiate the Divine mercy.'[2] With Taylor, Johnson argued that the oblation in the eucharist cannot be separated from the once-for-all sacrifice on the Cross. 'The distinguishing the oblation in the Eucharist from that on the cross, and that afterwards performed in heaven, is really a confounding or obscuring the whole mystery, and rendering it perplexed and intricate.'[3] And again, 'He finish'd the Sacrifice of Himself by entering as a High-Priest into Heaven, the true Holy of Holies, and He gives his life to our Sacrifice, by always appearing there in the Presence of God for us.'[4] Thus Christ is offered in the eucharist not materially but no less really, 'in mystery and effect'. With Johnson's tradition became linked the four 'usages' which the Nonjurors write into their liturgy of 1718: the mixture of wine and water in the chalice; the epiclesis upon the elements; a prayer of oblation to emphasize the sacrificial nature of the eucharist; and prayer for the dead.

Associated with the offertory oblation is the church's ancient practice of offering the bread and wine for the communion upon the altar, saying, 'Lord, we offer thee thy own, out of what thou hast bountifully given us.' Wheatly links this tradition to the rubric, *'the priest is then also to place upon the table so much bread and wine as he shall think sufficient'*, which, he points out (following Patrick), was added to the liturgy at the same time as the word *oblations* in the following prayer. The restored tradition had originally been enjoined by the 1549 liturgy but omitted in 1552 ('thrown out, I suppose, at the instance of Bucer and Martyr'); its reinstitution, Wheatly believes, was due to the influence of the writings of Joseph Mead (or Mede), in particular his *Christian Sacrifice*, where he exposed the defectiveness of the Anglican liturgy in this regard.[5] As Mead argued, the significance of

---

[1] Symon Patrick, *The Christian Sacrifice*, in his *Works* (Clarendon Press, Oxford, 1858) I, pp.376–377. John Dowden cogently argues that the revisers in 1661 meant by 'oblations' only 'alms and other money offerings for pious uses', and that Patrick's interpretation (followed by Johnson, Wheatly, and the Nonjurors), was a personal inference informed by knowledge of and attraction to the practice of the early church. John Dowden, 'What is the Meaning of "Our Alms and Oblations"? An Historical Study' in *Further Studies in the Prayer Book* (Methuen & Co., London, 1906) pp.176–222. On Patrick see also Stevenson, *Covenant of Grace*, pp.149–160.

[2] Johnson, *Unbloody Sacrifice* i, pp.304–305.

[3] Johnson, *Unbloody Sacrifice*, i, p.145.

[4] *Ibid.* ii, p.39.

[5] Wheatley, *Rational Illustration* ch.VI, Sect.X.§2.III, pp.238–9. Mead (1586–1638), a biblical scholar of Christ's College, Cambridge, is a mysterious figure in this context. Although writers such as Wheatly, Johnson, and Bull frequently cite him, his influence has not been explored in modern secondary literature. The title of another of his works, *Of the Name Altar, or θυσιαστηριον* (1635) is also suggestive of the direction of his thinking.

this offertory oblation of the elements was best understood by the early church: 'After which they received them, as it were, from him again, in order to convert them into the sacred banquet of the body and blood of his dear Son.'[1]

Robert Nelson in another popular manual, his *Companion for the Feasts and Fasts of the Church of England* (1704), summarizes the sacrificial significance of the oblation in his explanation of the end and design of the eucharist:

'To be the *Christian Sacrifice*, wherein Bread and Wine are offered to God, to acknowledge him Lord of the Creatures; and accordingly, in the *ancient Church*, they were laid on the Table by the Priest, as they are still ordered to be done by the *Rubric* in the Church of England, and tendered to God by this short Prayer, *Lord we offer thy own of what thou hast bountifully given us*; which, by *Consecration*, being made *Symbols* of the *Body* and *Blood of Christ*, we thereby represent to God the Father, the Passion of his Son . . . [even as] *Christ intercedes* continually for us in Heaven, by *presenting* his Death and Satisfaction to his Father . . . .'[2]

Because of the sacrificial aspect of the oblation Wheatly insisted that only the priest might place the elements on the altar, and not the clerk or sexton before morning prayer.[3] Another contemporary commentator, William Nicholls, was anxious to play down the sacrificial significance of the act but was no less adamant that only a priest should perform it.[4]

Waterland, on the other hand, was dissatisfied with Johnson's notions of material sacrifice even while maintaining a strong doctrine of sacrifice. He wrote, 'The Eucharist is both a true and a proper sacrifice, and the noblest that can be offered, as comprehending under it many true and evangelical sacrifices': the sacrifice of alms and oblations; of prayer; of praise and thanksgiving; of a penitent and contrite heart; of our selves, our souls and bodies; of Christ's mystical Body, the Church; of true converts and penitents by their pastors; and of faith, hope, and self-humiliation, commemorating and depending on Christ's once-for-all sacrifice. The sacrifice of Christ's Body the Church might be interpreted as implying the sacrifice of Christ in each eucharist, but Waterland discountenanced the idea of the sacrifice 'of the real body of Christ', or any material sacrifice.[5]

Despite Waterland's arguments, among those familiar with the eucharistic doctrine of the Eastern churches, the lack of an oblation was acutely felt (indeed the lack remains to this day in the ASB despite its presence in the Scottish and derivative rites). Lancelot Andrewes privately recited his own prayer of oblation drawn from Eastern sources.[6] The one defective aspect of the 1662 rite Wheatly does not even try to explain away or excuse was the dislocation of the prayer of oblation to the post-communion while it was the practice of the primitive Christians (and the 1549 and Scottish rites) to use such a prayer during the consecration itself: 'For the holy Eucharist was, from the very first institution, esteemed and received as a proper sacrifice, and solemnly offered to God upon the altar, before it was received and partaken of by the communicants.' In this instance, it is hard to avoid the suspicion that Wheatly encourages priests to recite the prayer of oblation before the

---

[1] *Ibid.*

[2] Robert Nelson, *Companion for the Feasts and Fasts of the Church of England: with Collects and Prayers for Each Solemnity* 36th ed. (London, 1826) p.475.

[3] Wheatly, *Rational Illustration* chap.VI, Sect.X, §2, p.239.

[4] Nicholls, *A Comment* p.ix.

[5] Waterland, *A Review,* pp.311–312.

[6] Stuhlman, *Eucharistic Celebration*, pp.23–25.

communion; he appeals to the example of Bishop Overall (1560-1619), whose practice it was to use the prayer of oblation 'between the Consecration and Administering, even when it was otherwise ordered by the public Liturgy'.[1]

Following on this primitive understanding of oblation, it was appropriate that contemporary Anglican congregations should, after the manner of the primitive church, leave their places in the nave to gather around the altar (Ills. 1, 3b). As Wheatly describes it, following the exhortation,

'The feast being now ready, and the guests prepared with due instruction, the Priest (who is the steward of those mysteries) invites them to *draw near*; thereby putting them in mind, that they are now invited into Christ's more special presence, to sit down with him at his own table.'[2]

The origin of this movement to the altar in the Anglican tradition is in the rubric of the 1549 Prayer Book instructing the congregation to bring forward their alms to the chancel: '*Then so manye as shalbe partakers of the holy Communion, shall tary still in the quire, or some conuenient place, nigh the quire, the men on the one side and the women on the other syde.*' As we have seen in his comments on the offertory, Wheatly was aware that this was the practice of the primitive church. Joseph Bingham also affirms that such movement was the practice of the early church, and he explicitly links the structure of the early eucharist to the Anglican by calling the Missa catechumenorum 'the Ante-Communion Service on the *Lord's Day*' held in the nave, and the Missa fidelium the 'Communion Service' celebrated at the altar.[3] Whether the practice initiated in 1549 of going to the chancel was a conscious or unconscious reflection of primitive styles of worship, it is worth emphasizing how close the practice (as well as the theology) of the early and modern periods was.

One churchman, Sir George Wheler, went so far as to suggest that this division of the service might be an effective way to reintegrate into the Church of England 'Penitents & those Dissenting on grounds of Discipline & Form of Worship' yet who would be willing to hear the scriptures and sermons. If the sermons were held at covenient times, they might be invited 'to come and be Our Auditors, for their further Instruction, concerning both Themselves and Us.'[4] If the Dissenters were to play the part of the primitive penitents, in the role of the Catechumeni would be the Quakers and others needing instruction; they would need such sermons as were usually preached to children. Needless to say, none of these could be admitted to the Holy Mysteries, but they might still be edified. Wheler argued that cathedrals and churches could be rearranged on a primitive pattern to serve

---

[1] Wheatley, *Rational Illustration* ch.VI, Sect.xxii, §3, pp.257–8. This was the practice also of Overall's chaplain John Cosin, a practice which, according to Stevenson, others adopted. (Stevenson, *Covenant* p.94).

[2] Wheatly, *Rational Illustration*, Chap.VI, Sect. XIV, p.247.

[3] Bingham, *Orig. Eccles.* Bk. XIV, chap.V, Sects. xii–xiii (*Works* I, 723–4) and Bk. XV, chap. III, Sect. v (*Works* I, 748). Although Bingham is not chiefly concerned, as is Wheatly, to point out every discrepancy between Anglican practice and that of the early church, he clearly (as above) relates primitive to current practice by translating Greek liturgical terms into English using terminology from the Prayer Book; he lets the discrepancies speak for themselves, hoping that by 'Preserving the Purity of the Primitive Faith', he might aid in 'Renewing the Spirit of the Antient Discipline and Primitive Practice' (Bingham, *Works* I, n.p. Dedication.)

[4] Sir George Wheler, *An Account of the Churches, or Places of Assembly, of the Primitive Christians; From the Churches of Tyre, Jerusalem, and Constantinople, Described by Eusebius. And Ocular Observations of Several very Ancient Edifices of Churches yet Extant in those Parts. With a Seasonable Application.* (S. Roycroft, London, 1689) pp.110–111.

such a ministry, with the pulpit moved to the place of the throne behind the altar, the clergy within the sanctuary, the Faithful (segregated by sex) within the choir, and the Dissenters in the aisles.[1]

One other comment in Wheatly impinges on the architectural setting of the eucharist. In the context of a discussion of the first of the set of rubrics at the conclusion of the communion office (on saying *at least* morning prayer and the ante-communion on all Sundays and holy days), he takes the opportunity to laud the practice of daily communion in the early church. Such, however, was not the practice of the Church of England even if it was the standard which the Prayer Book presumed. As Bingham lamented, 'The Churches are crowded to hear the Sermon, but when the time of the Holy Mysteries comes, they are empty and deserted.'[2] In order to encourage the people to communicate more frequently, Wheatly urges ministers to say the 'altar prayers' actually at the altar (even though 'I know indeed it is very frequently performed in the desk'), 'that the Church may still shew her readiness to administer the sacrament upon these days; and as that it is not hers nor the Minister's, but the people's fault, if it be not administered.'[3] Nicholls likewise defends the reading of the ante-communion 'that the Minister might shew his Readiness to do his Duty, if the People were not forward to do theirs'. He also notes the similarity of such a practice to the Missa catechumenorum of the early church, where those not baptized departed after the ministry of the Word.[4]

While the Church of England today is accustomed to recognizing the existence of widely divergent theologies of the eucharist, it is important to recognize that the theologies discussed here were peculiar neither to the early part of the eighteenth century nor to the high church party. Wheatly's commentary was a standard work. Bishop Thomas Wilson's *Short and Plain Instruction for a better understanding of the Sacrament* (24th ed. 1796) provided prayers of invocation of the Spirit and prayers for 'the whole mystical Body of Christ' for private use and interpreted oblation in a material sense, as did the perennially popular *Week's Preparation for a Worthy Receiving the Sacrament of the Lord's Supper* (38th ed. 1778).[5] Charles Daubeny, a leading high churchman at the end of the century, argued for Christ offered at each eucharist, and George Berkeley, Gloster Ridley, and the Hutchinsonians of the mid- to late century repeated Taylor's doctrine of sacrifice. Peter Nockles has observed that there continued to be a high demand for Nonjuror and 'virtualist' eucharistic literature throughout the eighteenth and early nineteenth centuries.[6] Waterland also remained influential:[7] the early nineteenth century bishop William Cleaver (himself a 'virtualist') maintained that receptionism held 'the most general suffrage among our divines' in the

---

[1] *Ibid.* pp.112–115.
[2] Bingham, *Orig. Eccles.* Bk. XV, chap. IX, Sect. viii (*Works* I, pp.830–831).
[3] Wheatly, *Rational Illustration* Ch.VI, Sect.xxx, pp.268–271. But see also A&E p.82 for the suggestion that 'The custom of reading Altar Prayers from the reading pew was only an extension and development of the contemporary Continental practice of singing the Epistle and Gospel from the ambos and could well be justified on the ground that it made for congregational worship.'
[4] Nicholls, *A Comment* n.p. [Of frequency of Communion]
[5] Sharp, 'New Perspectives', pp.11–13.
[6] Peter Nockles, *The Oxford Movement in Context: Anglican High Churchmanship, 1760–1857* (Cambridge University Press, Cambridge, 1994) p.237.
[7] F. C. Mather, *High Church Prophet. Bishop Samuel Horsley (1733–1806) and the Caroline Tradition in the Later Georgian Church* (Clarendon Press, Oxford, 1992) pp.18–20. Horsley himself was an enthusiast for the first Prayer Book of Edward VI and the Scottish rite. *Ibid.* pp.204–205.

eighteenth century.[1] Early Evangelicals were much influenced by the Nonjurors. John Wesley followed Daniel Brevint, the Restoration dean of Lincoln, in identifying the Holy Ghost as the agent of consecration and saw Christ's sacrifice as once-for-all but eternal 'through the eternal presence of the Victim-Priest before the eyes of the Father', the sacrifice in which we participate.[2] Wilson's *A Short and Plain Instruction* played a key part in Charles Simeon's conversion.[3] It would thus seem that the doctrines discussed here were the most widely held within the Church, challenged only by those who with Benjamin Hoadly (*A Plain Account of the Nature and End of the Sacrament of the Lord's Supper*, 1735) saw the sacrament as merely commemorative.[4] Although it has been argued, particularly by Dugmore, that Waterland's theology represents the true Anglican *via media* theology of the eucharist and that Johnson's theology was popular only with Nonjurors,[5] this brief glance at some commentators on the Prayer Book may call this assessment into question. In view of the high doctrine of presence, sacrifice, epiclesis on the elements, and oblation expressed in such perennially popular and standard commentators as Wheatly, Nelson, and Wilson, it must be questioned whether the influence of Johnson and others of his school has been underestimated. Even so, it is important not to assume that the schools discussed here were bitterly divided by their differences. Wheatly assured the Nonjuring primus Thomas Brett that Waterland 'really maintains the sacrifice as we do, but expresses himself in a different manner'.[6] Waterland himself maintained that the two positions were divided only by a 'difference of words or names, arising chiefly from the difficulty of determining what sacrifice properly means'.[7]

Before proceeding to an examination of church architecture itself, it is worth while drawing out some of the architectural implications of the doctrine of the eucharist. First, it ought to be clear that the eighteenth century took eucharistic theology very seriously. Today a parish which celebrated the eucharist but once a month might be thought to devalue the sacrament, but for the eighteenth century the evidence suggests otherwise: the popularity of such preparation manuals as Wilson's *Short and Plain Instruction* and the *Week's Preparation* indicate that these Anglicans approached the sacrament (if less frequently than is common today) with great devotion. Because of the emphasis in Anglican theology on eucharistic sacrifice, the holy table was frequently called the altar, and in the Laudian period there was much debate on the most proper setting for it. Laud's own eucharistic theology was more moderate than that of Andrewes, yet he saw the altar 'as the greatest place of God's residence upon earth.'[8] At the Restoration, Laud's campaign for the railed altar at the east end was vindicated. But, we must ask, did the setting otherwise match the theology? Architecturally speaking, we should expect a setting worthy of the sacrament, of a realization of the real presence of Christ and of the re-presentation of his sacrifice, indeed a setting for the counterpart of the heavenly altar where Christ eternally pleads his sacrifice before the Father.

---

[1] Nockles, *Oxford Movement* p.237.
[2] Christopher J. Cocksworth, *Evangelical Eucharistic Thought in the Church of England* (Cambridge University Press, Cambridge, 1993) pp.67–69. On Brevint, see Stevenson, *Covenant of Grace*, pp.98–107.
[3] *Ibid.* p.63.
[4] For an account of Hoadly as well as further information about popular devotional manuals, see Stone, *A History* ii, ch.xv, pt II, §§ii, vi, vii.
[5] Dugmore, *Eucharistic Doctrine*, pp.182–183.
[6] Wheatly to Brett 31 October 1739, cited in H.Broxap, *The Later Nonjurors*, p.212.
[7] Waterland, *A Review*, p.309.
[8] *Anglicanism* no. 275, p.608.

3. Church Architecture in Relation to the Eucharist

How, then, did contemporary church architecture give expression to the theology of the eucharist as we have seen it articulated? The requirements of the canons were rudimentary: Canon LXXXVII demanded that the Holy Table be placed where it was most convenient for celebration, be covered with a decent carpet or covering, and that the tables of the Decalogue be set up at the east end. In the late seventeenth and eighteenth centuries, however, the setting tended to be much more elaborate. The importance of the eucharist was emphasized in a number of ways—the division between nave and chancel, sometimes with a chancel screen; the altar being railed off and raised up one or more steps; the painting of the chancel ceiling or the area above the altar; the presence of a ciborium or a painted canopy over the altar; the presence of a reredos or large east window above the altar; and the rich furnishing of the table itself with a cloth, communion plate, and sometimes candles. The eighteenth-century church valued its chancels and strove the beautify them; if the work done was ordinarily in a classical style which to modern eyes clashes with mediaeval settings, the intent was nevertheless to honour and adorn the celebration of the eucharist, to give it a worthy setting according to the taste of the time.

Although the Church of England suffered its share of iconoclasm in the Reformation, the church buildings (if not furnishings) survived the period relatively intact, at least in part because the chancels remained in use for the celebration of the eucharist. Addleshaw and Etchells sum up the adaptation of mediaeval churches for Anglican worship as being ruled by the primitive pattern of movement between the ministries of Word and Sacrament: 'The process by which mediaeval churches were adapted for Prayer Book worship might be summed up as one of taking the communicants into the chancel for the Eucharist, so that they can be within sight and hearing of the priest at the altar; and of bringing down the priest from the chancel into the nave so that he could be amongst his people for Morning and Evening Prayer.'[1] Even when church design was rationalized into single-room 'auditory' churches, the same sense of movement would usually remain. Horton Davies emphasizes the importance of the sense of different worship spaces or areas: 'Moving to the chancel for the Communion service seemed to give the Sacrament a special sacredness, which has been strongly emphasized through most of Anglican history; the chancel screen helped to separate the liturgy of the catechumens from the liturgy of the faithful, thus imparting to the climax of worship a sense of deep mystery.'[2]

Elizabeth I's Order of October 1561 had made it quite clear that screens (without roods) were to remain in churches, and the practice of building churches with screened chancels

---

[1] A&E p.45

[2] Horton Davies, *Worship and Theology in England. From Cranmer to Hooker 1534–1603* (Princeton University Press, Princeton, 1970) p.365.

never entirely ceased; although Wren in London tended to build single-cell churches, at the insistence of the then rector William Beveridge, St Peter's Cornhill (1681) was given a chancel and chancel screen. Beveridge explained his rationale in his sermon at the church's opening:

'The Sacrament of the Lord's Supper being the highest mystery in all our religion, as representing the death of the Son of God to us, hence that place where this Sacrament is administered was always made and reputed the highest place in the church. . . . And that this place being appropriated to the Sacrament of the Lord's Supper, it ought to be contrived, as may be most convenient for those who are to partake of that blessed ordinance. But it must needs be more convenient for those who are to enjoy communion with Christ, and in Him with one another, in this Holy Sacrament, to meet together as one body, in one place separated for that purpose, than to be dispersed, as otherwise they would be, some in one and some in another part of the church; or, in short, it is much better for the place to be separate than the people.'[1]

Worship in the chancel heightens the communicants' sense of themselves as the Body of Christ. Screens continued to be erected in churches down to the beginning of the nineteenth century; although screens were sometimes lowered, they were rarely entirely removed.[2]

It must be added that normally the royal arms were placed on top of the screen, on the tympanum, or over the altar in an auditory church, the arms first appearing in churches under Henry VIII. Although their presence may now seem inappropriate, symbolizing as it were the need to partake of the sacrament as a qualification for full citizenship and office, it is important not to see them as an emblem of Erastianism, of the state domination of the church. As Addleshaw and Etchells point out, the royal supremacy indicated no power external to the church; the king was no purely secular person but what was known to the seventeenth century as a 'spiritual person', anointed and clothed in a dalmatic at his coronation and therefore, though not ordained, capable of jurisdiction in spiritual matters.[3]

'When the royal arms, the Commandments, the Belief, and the Lord's Prayers with explanatory sentences from scripture were all painted on the tympanum, and perhaps too the letters IHS at the top, the whole scheme spoke to the parishioners of the duties incumbent upon them as members both of an earthly and a heavenly city.'[4]

One of the aspects of eighteenth century church buildings which has led critics to accuse contemporary Anglicans of devaluing the eucharist has been the towering reading desk and pulpit (double- or triple-decker), which was occasionally found in the central aisle, thus obscuring the view of the altar. Very few churches have left them in this position in England: one survives at King's Norton, Leics.,[5] and there is another notable and beautiful

---

[1] William Beveridge, Sermon preached at the opening of St Peter's, Cornhill, 1681, in Vernon Staley, ed. *Hierurgia Anglicana* (De la More Press, London, 1902) I, pp.23–24. Also in Beveridge *Works* (Library of Anglo–Catholic Theology) vi, p.388.

[2] For a history of screens from the Reformation see Aymer Vallance, *English Church Screens, being Great Roods, Screenwork & Rood–lofts of Parish Churches in England and Wales* (B. T. Batsford, London, 1936) chap. x.

[3] See, for example, John Godolphin, *Repertorium Canonicum: or, an Abridgment of the Ecclesiastical Laws of this Realm, Consistent with the Temporal* 3rd ed. (London, 1687) p.9.

[4] A&E pp.101–104. The authors also point out that the prominent presence of the royal arms was not peculiar to British churches. See pp.152–153 for the arrangements in Lyons Cathedral.

[5] On this church, see Mark Chatfield, *Churches the Victorians Forgot* (Moorland Publishing, 1989) pp.68–71.

example of this type at Trinity Church in Newport, Rhode Island. Stephen Dorsey has suggested that the pulpit in such a position indicated no irreverence for the altar, rather it preserved the mediaeval idea of the compartmented church with a separate chancel into which (according to Anglican practice) the communicants would draw near.[1] It is, however, even more illuminating to look to the example of the early church, where the ambo performed precisely the same function as the reading desk (the sermon itself was probably usually preached from the bishop's throne behind the altar). Bingham points out, 'The *Ambo* itself was what we now call the Reading-Desk, a Place made on Purpose for the Readers and Singers, and such of the Clergy as ministered in the first Service, called Missa Catechumenorum.'[2] In Anglican services, the minister and the parish clerk performed these same functions. And, as may be seen in the plates from Bingham (Ill. 2), the ambo was normally placed in the centre, directly opposite the bema and altar. Beveridge comments on his own *Ichnographia Templorum* (his reconstruction based on textual evidence, not an archaeological reconstruction), 'Hunc autem, et de eo prius aliqua delibimus, in medio Ecclesiæ interspeciosas & sanctas fores, & altari directè oppositum esse.' His illustration is 'fidem facit Symeon Thessalonicensis dicens, ὁ ἄμβων πρὸ τῆς θύρας τοῦ μνήματος ἵσταται, Ambon è conspectu parte bematis statuitur. . . .'[3] Sometimes, as at All Saints, Derby, in 1723–5, the pulpit was placed in the middle to increase seating capacity; but here there was no neglect of the eucharist, for at the same time wrought iron chancel screens and a marble altar were installed![4]

Within the chancel (or within the sanctuary of an auditory church) the altar was usually railed in at the east end (not always so, as we have seen in Wheatly's concern about holy tables within the body of the church). Nicholls recounts how this arrangement came to prevail:

> 'Since the Restoration, no positive determination being made, in the review of the Common Prayer, the dispute has very happily died; and the tables have generally been set altar-wise, and railed in, without any opposition thereto; the generality of all parishioners esteeming it a very decent situation, they coming of themselves to a good liking of it, which they could not be brought to, by the too rigid methods which were heretofore used.'[5]

---

[1] Stephen P. Dorsey, *Early English Churches in America 1607–1807* (Oxford University Press, New York, 1952) p.27.

[2] Bingham, *Orig. Eccles* Bk. VIII, Chap. V, Sect. iv (*Works* I, p.293). As Addleshaw and Etchells point out (p.82), the Elizabethan bishops probably did not have the ambo in mind when they devised the reading desk; this would seem to be a serendipitous conformity to the primitive church.

[3] William Beveridge, Συνοδικόν, *sive Pandectæ Canonum SS. Apostolorum, et Conciliorum ab Ecclesia Græca receptorum* (Oxonii, E Theatro Sheldoniano) 1672, II, Annotationes, p.73. Simeon of Thessalonica (a fifteenth-century Byzantine ecclosiologist) *de Sacram* (Migne P.G. clv, p.345). For more on the reading pew as ambo see A&E, pp.82–83.

[4] Basil F. L. Clarke, *The Building of the Eighteenth-Century Church* (London, S.P.C.K.) 1963, p.169. In 1726 the pulpit was moved to the south pillar. Then, in 1873 the pulpit was moved back to the centre and the marble altar was replaced by a wooden table; the marble mensa was displayed in the church with a pointed (and entirely misplaced) quotation from Bishop Ridley about 'the old superstitious opinions of the popish mass'!

[5] Nicholls, *Comment*, n.p. [On the Ornaments Rubric]

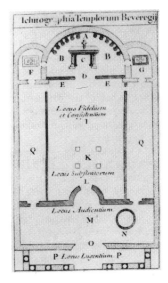

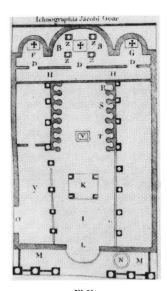

Ill. 2a   Ill.2b

Ichnographia Templorum Orientalium, from Joseph Bingham, *Origines Ecclesiasticæ* (1708-22).

B. *S. Bema* C. *Altare* E. *Cancelli Bematis* F. *Prothesis* G. *Diaconicum* K. *Ambo* N. *Baptisterium* Z. *Ciborium.*

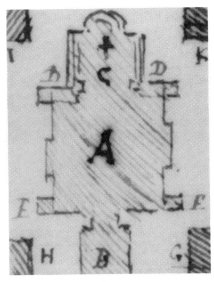

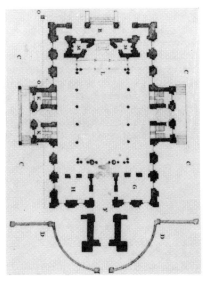

Ill. 2c   Ill. 2d

Nicholas Hawksmoor, 'The Basilica after the Primitive Christians' (c.1712)
A. 'The Church East and West' B. Font
C. 'The Chancelli' D. 'The Vestrys for the Sacred Robes and holy Vessells'

Nicholas Hawksmoor, 'Basilica Grenovicana', St. Alphege, Greenwich, 1712-18, engraved Johannes Kip.
G. *Baptisterium* L. *Cancelli, inter Ecclesiam et Sacrarium* M. *Sacrarium* M. *Sacristæ duæ*

Church Architecture in Relation to the Eucharist   29

During the period, the rails were usually returned to the east wall. (See Ill. 4c.) This had the effect of enabling more communicants to gather around the altar.[1]

The tables of the decalogue were already affixed to the east wall, but with the altar there permanently, the east wall of the church became the obvious place to focus decoration that interpreted or in some other way brought out the significance of the eucharist. Addleshaw and Etchells maintain, 'There was one wall which even in the poorest of parishes was almost invariably decorated, and that was the east one, whether the whole of it or the part in the centre, in order to mark the proper place for the altar and form a reredos.'[2] Altarpiece paintings were widely used and appreciated. As Archbishop William Wake (1657-1737) noted in his *Exposition of the Doctrine of the Church of England,*

'When the Pictures of God the FATHER, and of the HOLY GHOST, so directly contrary both to the second Commandment and to SAINT PAUL'S Doctrine, shall be taken away, and those of our SAVIOUR and the blessed SAINTS be by all necessary Cautions rendered truly the BOOKS and not the SNARES of the Ignorant, then will we respect the Images of our SAVIOUR and the blessed VIRGIN. And as some of us now bow down before the Altar, and all of us are enjoined to do so at the Name of the LORD JESUS; so will we not fail to testify all due Respect to his Representation.'[3]

The most usual form of reredos incorporated the decalogue in the middle with the Apostles' Creed and the Lord's Prayer on either side. Further decoration could be simple or elaborate, with a glory, an IHS, tetragrammaton, pictures or statues of Moses and Aaron or St Peter and St John. Moses and Aaron were so popularly used that one writer referred to them as 'the two faithful prophets ever attendant on our altars'. Like the royal arms, they were a reminder of State and Church, magistracy and ministry.[4] 'Moses is usually represented in the robe of a prophet, and Aaron in the vestments of a high priest as they are described in Exodus. He is always waving a censer; and in Bristol Cathedral he was raised to the cardinalate and given a red hat.'[5]

Sometimes large paintings were used as a reredos. In 1755 St Mary Redcliffe in Bristol spent £500 on three pictures by Hogarth—an Ascension over the east window, the three Marys at the sepulchre on one side and the high priests' servants sealing the stone on the other. In 1792, the raising of Jairus' daughter was added.[6] There are also examples of remarkably abstract altar paintings, notably that of the divine glory in St Michael's, Framlingham, Suffolk.

Wealthy parishes would spare no expense in erecting altarpieces, which could be baroque in their ostentation. On 19 May 1739 a faculty was granted the parishioners of St Michael

---

[1] A&E pp.162–4.

[2] A&E p.157.

[3] Cited in [Thomas Wilson,] *The Ornaments of Churches Considered, with a particular View of the late Decoration of the Parish Church of St Margaret Westminster* (W. Jackson, Oxford, 1761) p.28.

[4] For the popularity of this theme in Restoration England, see John Spurr, *The Restoration Church of England, 1646–1689* (Yale University Press, New Haven, 1991) pp.48, 59–60.

[5] A&E p.161. See footnote 3 for locations of images of Moses and Aaron.

[6] A&E p.158. For descriptions of further altar paintings and their sometimes highly political subject matter, see Wickham Legg, *English Church Life*, pp.129-33.

Agite, veneremur supplices, flexis ante Dominum
Creatorem nostrum genibus. PSAL. XCV. 6.

Ill. 3a
Frontispiece to Thomas Parsell's
Latin Prayer Book (1713)

Ill. 3b
Frontispiece to *The Divine
Banquet, or Sacramental
Devotions (1700)*

Church Architecture in Relation to the Eucharist   31

Coslany, Norwich,

> 'to erect an altarpiece 18 ft. high, divided into five parts or panels, and painted with the Resurrection in the middle panel, and the four Evangelists as witnesses of the Resurrection. On each side of the middle of the panel there was to be a Corinthian column to support an open pediment, on which was to stand, carved on a pedestal, a pelican; and round the top part seven golden candlesticks with other ornaments.'[1]

The pelican in her piety, feeding her children with her own blood, was a popular symbol of the eucharist; there is a fine example in the Grinling Gibbons altarpiece at St James's Picadilly. The seven golden candlesticks in Rev. 1.13 are a sign of the presence of the Son of Man.[2]

An even more magnificent structure was to be found in the 1703 altar-piece at St Saviour's, Southwark, which was 35 ft. high:

> 'It consists of an upper and lower part; the latter is adorned with four fluted columns, and their entablature of the Corinthian order; the inter-columns are the Commandments done in black letters, on large slabs of white and veined marble, under a glory (exhibiting the name *Jehovah*, in Hebrew characters) and the triangular pediments, between four attic pilasters, with an acroteria of the figures of seven golden candlesticks replenished with tapers; the whole is under a spacious circular pediments belonging to the Corinthian columns, which are placed between the Paternoster and Creed; each under a pediment, between small pilasters. . . . In the centre of this upper part is a glory in the shape of a dove descending within a circular group of cherubims, all very spacious and finely painted . . . .'[3]

This reredos is an overwhelming expression of the identity of earthly and heavenly worship, of the church militant and church triumphant, in the eucharist. The glory with the tetragrammaton indicates the Shekinah (doxa) and is emblemmatic of the divine (real) presence; the golden candlesticks and cherubim remind one of the presence of the 'angels and archangels and all the company of heaven'. And mindful of the debates in eucharistic theology, the presence of the dove descending is particularly notable. We know that the early church held consecration to be primarily by the Holy Ghost invoked in the epiclesis upon the elements, and in some early churches 'the Holy Ghost was represented in the effigies of a silver Dove hovering over the Altar', the *peristerion* or *columbae*.[4] The presence of a dove over the altar in St Saviour's indicates adherence to this primitive eucharistic doctrine.[5]

The other interesting feature in these two altar pieces is the columns supporting pediments. These are expressly columns, not pilasters, so they must be supporting a structure projecting over the altar from the wall of the reredos. This structure is a version

---

[1] Clarke, *Building* p.163. Clarke asserts this was typical of the more elaborate altarpieces.

[2] A surviving example (from 1728) of the seven candlesticks may be found at Gayhurst, Bucks.: see fig. 38 in Whiffen, *Stuart and Georgian Churches*. On the church see also, Chatfield, *Churches the Victorians Forgot*, pp.13-15.

[3] Clarke, *Building* p.166, citing David Hughson, *A History and Description of London, Westminster and Southwark* vol. iv p.498. See also Wickham Legg, *English Church Life* p.128 for a 1708 description of an equally impressive altarpiece at All Hallows Lombard Street.

[4] Bingham, *Orig. Eccles.* Bk. VIII, Chap. VI, Sect. xix (*Works* i, pp.303-304).

[5] Other doves are to be found e.g. in the reredos or above the altar at St.Werburgh's, Dublin (A&E p.159 ft. 5); Trinity College Chapel, Oxford; St Peter's, Vere Street (the Marylebone Chapel); and St Vedast Foster Lane, St Clement Eastcheap, St Martin Ludgate, and St Mary Woolnoth, all in the City of London.

of the ciborium, which Bingham describes as a 'Canopy hanging over the Altar . . . in the form of a little Turret upon four pillars at each corner of the Altar'.[1] Wren designed a full ciborium for the high altar of St Paul's 'consisting of four Pillars wreathed, of the richest *Greek* marbles, supporting a canopy hemispherical, with proper Decorations of Architecture and Sculpture,'[2] and in the early eighteenth century one was set up in the chapel of Trinity College, Cambridge.[3] The altar at St Michael's Cornhill had a canopy with a remarkable set of symbolic decorations relating to the eucharist:

> 'On the N. and S. sides of the Altar is a spacious Pieddroit, and another on the S. side painted, and a Chalice, Paten, Incense pot, *Aaron's* budded Rod, and the Pot of Manna, *etc.* painted; and on the Roof over the Table, is a Glory appearing in the Clouds, painted and gilt, some of whose Rays are about 8 Foot in length.'[4]

Trinity College Chapel, Oxford, has a projecting pediment like those in London and Norwich, resting on two Corinthian columns and forming a ciborium. (It has already been noted that at Zerzita there was a two–column ciborium.[5]) This altarpiece is one of the finest remaining examples of its type and is truly astonishing in its wealth of detail.[6] The chancel is raised three steps above the choir. The altar was originally more nearly square and the returns of the rails came inside the Corinthian columns. In the central panel of the reredos is a glory in inlaid wood; the lighter-colored fruitwood carving around the edge includes bunches of grapes and ears of wheat (oblation), the instruments of the passion (sacrifice) and the old chapel; at the top of the central panel is a large chalice upheld by winged cherubs and overflowing with grapes (unity of earth and heaven in the eucharist). Two Corinthian columns hold up a broken round-headed pediment (ciborium) surmounted by two angels. Directly above the altar at the curve of the coving, is a dove descending; the pediment is broken in such a way as if to open a path between the dove and the altar, thus emphasizing the role of the Spirit in the consecration. This sanctuary might be seen as a summary statement of the Anglican-patristic doctrine of the eucharist.

Illustrations of other altars with ciboria (only the columns are visible and not the pediment or canopy) are in Wheatly and Lancelot Addison's *An Introduction to the Sacrament* (4th ed., 1693) (Ill. 1 and cover ill.).[7] Those altar pieces without columns but with engaged columns or pilasters supporting a pediment also express a ciborium, but in a simpler and less expensive way. For example, the reredos at St Katherine, Chiselhampton, Oxon. (1763) (Ill. 4c), is surmounted with a pediment, and altar and reredos are set within a proscenium

---

[1] Bingham, *Orig. Eccles.* Bk. VIII, Chap. VI, Sect. xviii (*Works* I, p.303).

[2] Christopher Wren, ed. *Parentalia: or Memoirs of the Family of the Wrens...* (London, 1750) 292, ft. 9. The ciborium was not erected because satisfactory marbles could not be found at the time.

[3] Ninian Comper, *Of the Atmosphere of a Church* (London, 1947) p.21. See also Robert Willis and John Willis Clark, *The Architectural History of the University of Cambridge* (Cambridge, 1886) ii, 584-5. (I am indebted to the Revd Dr Arnold Browne, Dean of Chapel, Trinity College, for this reference).

[4] A description of 1708, cited in Wickham Legg, *English Church Life* p.129.

[5] Davies, *Early Christian Church Architecture* p.84.

[6] This decoration has neven been analysed in detail – its original 'Orthography and Ichnography' of 1691 has usually been ascribed to Henry Aldrich, Dean of Christ Church, and the carving of the various parts of the reredos to Gibbons, Maine, and Frogley. See W.G. Hiscock, *Henry Aldrich of Christ Church* (Oxford: Privately Printed) 1960, p.19.

[7] In the Addison note the candles burning on the altar during the sermon or exhortation and the 'primitive' segregation by sex; in the communion illustration note the ministers decently vested in surplices and the Shekinah of presence over the consecrated elements on the altar.

arch which may serve as a rudimentary ciborium. The reredos is a strikingly handsome piece, incorporating the decalogue, Our Father, and Creed; above the tables of the Law are winged cherub's heads and a glory (Shekinah) with tetragrammaton. This unpretentious country church is representative of the eighteenth century's concern with providing a worthy setting for worship even in simple country settings.[1]

Another important architectural feature emphasizing the altar and perhaps too often overlooked is the presence of large or distinctive east windows often in the form of Palladian windows or large round arched windows.[2] Such windows are noticably absent only in Wren's City churches, where irregular sites ensured that fenestration was primarily a function of the need for light. East windows focussed a stream of light on the focal point of the altar; Friary draws an interesting parallel to continental Baroque efforts to focus light and attention on the altar.[3] He is perhaps on shakier ground when he speculates on the relation between such windows and the theology of light as divine in some of the Cambridge Platonists, who 'seemed to equate the sun with a sort of world soul which is the principle of life and of living forms, the creating and generating force in all living processes'.[4] Such ideas have no apparent relation to Christian worship. The patristic focus on the expectation of the parousia, the eastward orientation towards the rising sun of the Resurrection, is a more demonstrable and fitting influence on church building. Peter King cites Tertullian in a passage which incorporates nicely both the figure of light and the parousia: 'The House of our Dove-like Religion is simple, built on high and in open View, respecting the Light as the Figure of the Holy Spirit, and the East as the representation of Christ.'[5]

It is worth noting that in churches with no chancel or apse, the distinctive east window may be seen as an externally visible sign of the importance of the eucharist. Indeed, such a window is usually the only external indication of any of the activities that go on within a church—neither baptism nor the ministry of the word has such an external indicator. Nonconformist (and a few Anglican) churches usually had the pulpit where the Anglican altar was found; in each case, a distinctive window said, 'This is what we do here.'

The altar itself, whether called the table, the holy table, the altar table, or the altar, was usually small and nearly square. Even where there was no shortage of space, 'churchmen often preferred small altars because they were the rule in the early Church.'[6] They might be either of wood or of stone, no doctrinal significance being attached to either material[7], but wooden altars were sometimes elaborately carved. A very fine example of this is the altar (recently tragically stolen) belonging to St Andrew's Wheatfield, Oxon., carved with

---

[1] The register for the church's consecration on 27 August 1763 notes that all was done decently and in order. Clarke, *Building*, p.183.

[2] The only extended discussion of the significance of these windows is to be found in Donald Richard Friary, 'The Architecture of the Anglican Church in the Northern American Colonies: A Study of Religious, Social and Cultural Expression' Unpublished Ph.D. dissertation, University of Pennsylvania, 1971, chap. VII.

[3] *Ibid.* p.254.

[4] *Ibid.* pp.264ff.

[5] King, *Enquiry*, p.153, citing Justin's *Advers. Valent.*

[6] A&E p.166. There is unfortunately no reference for this statement. Bingham writes copiously about early altars but says nothing about size or shape.

[7] For Bingham's affirmation of this in relation to the early church, *Orig. Eccles.* Bk. VIII, chap. VI, sect. xv (*Works* I, p.302). For examples of stone altars, see Wickham Legg, *English Church Life*, 134-36.

a cherub, wheat sheaves, and bunches of grapes.[1] Plain tables were usually covered with a cloth; all manner of colors and fine materials were used, although the most popular color seems to have been crimson. The frontal might be embroidered with an IHS, a glory, the instruments of the passion (as emblems of sacrifice), or the arms of the donor.[2] Candles might often be found on the tables, particularly in cathedrals and college chapels, although the chances that the candles might be lighted did decrease in the period under consideration.[3]

Architecturally speaking, thus far we have looked primarily at Anglican adaptations of existing mediaeval structures. What then do we find in churches built during this period and designed specifically for Anglican worship? Although Wren was a pioneer in this regard, the designs for the 'fifty new churches' called for by the Act of Parliament of 1711 are in some ways of greater interest. The bearing on the liturgy of the architectural aspects of the churches was carefully set out in advance, and in these principles the 'primitive' tradition in Anglicanism seen so clearly at work in liturgical thinking is also much in evidence. Furthermore, these principles were disseminated widely through James Gibbs's *Book of Architecture*, which provided the models for countless churches built throughout the English-speaking world.

First, with Wren, let us take a closer look at his letter on the auditory church and then relate it to what we know about him, his churches, and the performance of the liturgy in them. The principle guiding Wren in the building of his churches is that everyone present should be able to hear *and see:* 'In our reformed Religion, it would seem vain to make a *Parish-church* larger than that all who are present can both hear and see.' Furthermore, there was more for them to hear than the sermon: 'I can hardly think it practicable to make a single Room so capacious, with Pews and Galleries, as to hold above 2,000 Persons, and all to hear *the Service* [my emphasis], and both to hear distinctly, and see the Preacher.' As a model of these qualities he points to St James's Westminster (Picadilly), which he characterized as beautiful, convenient, and 'the cheapest of any Form I could invent'.[4] In the church as built the reading desk and pulpit stood in front of the the altar. Did Wren then devalue the altar and the eucharist? Not at all; the only place he would countenance using marble was in altarpieces, it being too costly for other uses. Addleshaw and Etchells observe, 'Much money and thought went to the furnishing of Wren churches with altars, communion rails, and altar-pieces.'[5] In some of his churches (e.g. St James Garlickhythe, St Edmund King and Martyr, St Bride Fleet Street, and St Clement Danes) the altar was further distinguished with a chancel recess or apse. But it is critical to remember the importance of a balanced presentation of the liturgy and the sense of liturgical movement in Anglican worship as in that of the early church. The font at the door, the central reading desk-pulpit (ambo), and the eastern altar are three stages in the Christian journey towards

---

[1] See Fig. 137 in Whiffen, *Stuart and Georgian Churches.*
[2] A&E pp.166–167.
[3] The evidence from texts and engravings indicating usage of altar lights is summarized in E.S. Roscoe, ed. *The Bishop of Lincoln's Case* p.189. In brief: 1681–1737, independent evidences of lighting in 11 or 12 cases; 1681–1737, none, or unlit, or lighted only for light, in 14 or 15 cases; 1750–1847, none are shown in 8 cases; 1750–1847, candles are shown in 11 cases. See also Wickham Legg, *English Church Life*, pp.139-44.
[4] A&E p.249.
[5] *Ibid.* p.56.

the eschaton; each has its own importance and dignity (epitomized in Ill. 3a). Furthermore, the altar would be seen fully by those communicants who draw near and kneel around the altar. The auditory church may be a single room, but its function cannot be taken in at a single glance. As Kerry Downes has observed, 'The ritual organization of Wren's church was separate from and less definite than the formal organization, and usually took precedence over it.'[1] And finally when one takes into consideration that the deeply religious Wren came from a staunchly high church clerical family (his father was the royalist Dean of Windsor and his uncle, Bishop Matthew Wren, was one of the most zealous Laudian bishops), that he moved primarily in high church circles, and that he was deeply attached to the cult of the Royal Martyr,[2] it becomes impossible to see any Wren church as the mere 'preaching box' usually implied by the term 'auditory'. His work for the most exacting Roman Catholic client was interchangeable with that for Anglicans: indeed, the elaborate altarpiece (1685-6) designed by Wren and carved by Grinling Gibbons for the triumphalist Roman Catholic James II's royal chapel at Whitehall became the high altar for Westminster Abbey.[3]

Taking all these factors into account, does it seem as if St Stephen Walbrook has been reordered appropriately? A short extract from architect Robert Potter's reflections on his work at St Stephen clearly reveals how far he absorbed the ethos of the Wren design and of contemporary Anglicanism: he delimits 'the general arrangement of the original furnishings [to] high box pews, a diminutive Sanctuary, and lofty Pulpit. Holy Communion was celebrated only infrequently and the building served primarily as an auditory for the Ministry of the Word' (i.e. preaching).[4] Potter in his re-ordering has taken the dome as his defining element—all attention is focused on the round Henry Moore altar under the dome.

Although he does not cite their influence, it may be that Potter's adaptation was influenced by the round Renaissance churches of diGiorgio, Leonardo, and Palladio, churches of which Wren almost certainly was aware. Many of Wren's plans for City churches, (e.g. St Stephen's, St Mary at Hill, St Anne and St Agnes, and St Martin Ludgate) were based on 'centralized' plans.[5] The Renaissance theorists' devotion to the centralized plan was based on a vision of divine harmony as expressed in geometric perfection and a delight in the centrality of man as the measure of all things.[6] But that horizontal sense of

---

[1] Kerry Downes, The Architecture of Wren (Granada, London, 1982) p.61.

[2] Wren drew up designs for a tomb for Charles I, 'Mausoleum Divi Caroli, Regii Martyris'. R.A. Bedard, 'Wren's mausoleum for Charles I and the cult of the Royal Martyr' in Architectural History 27 (1984) pp.36-47.

[3] For a description of the altarpiece see David Green, Grinling Gibbons. His Work as Carver and Statuary 1648-1721. (Country Life Ltd., London, 1964) pp.59-60. On its history at Westminster Abbey, see Jocelyn Perkins, Westminster Abbey; Its Worship and Ornaments. Alcuin Club Collections xxxiii. I, pp.65-81, 88-93. (Oxford University Press, London, 1938).

[4] 'Robert Potter reflects on his work at St Stephen's Church, Walbrook' in Church Building Winter/Spring 1988.

[5] See Margaret Whinney, Wren (Thames and Hudson, London, 1971) pp.61ff. for possible Dutch influence on these designs.

[6] Rudolf Wittkower, Architectural Principles in the Age of Humanism (Alec Tiranti, London, 1952), pp.11–15, 21-22. On the tension between the vertical and the horizontal in the early church architecture, see Davies, Early Christian Church Architecture pp.51–52.

journey towards the eschatological goal, from font to Word to heavenly banquet, which was typical of Anglican liturgical principles in their insistence on the font at the door, the eastern altar, and the movement from desk to altar, is negated by the exclusively central focus at St Stephen's. If, as Nicolaus Pevsner points out, the centralized church focuses on the human in control over the divine geometry as the 'measure of all things', then 'The religious meaning of the church is replaced by a human one. Man is in the church no longer pressing forward to reach the transcendental goal, but enjoying the beauty that surrounds him and the glorious sensation of being the centre of this beauty.'[1] It surely cannot be authentic to twentieth century Christianity to be seeking God in geometric perfection? God is present to us not in our control of geometric form, but in our pilgrim journey towards the realization of his kingdom. The re-ordering of St Stephen's cannot be seen as an appropriate approach to remodelling such churches.

We come next to a consideration of the plans for the Fifty New Churches of 1711. It must be said in advance that neither Addleshaw and Etchells nor Yates considers them in any detail in their books on Anglican architecture and worship. But more explicitly than any other churches, these few buildings (only twelve of the fifty were ever built) reveal the Anglican sense of identity with the primitive church. Advisers to the commission included some already encountered in this study, including Sir Peter King (author of the *Enquiry into . . . the Primitive Church*)[2] and (in a covert capacity) George Hickes. Pierre du Prey has established a direct connection between the patristic scholarship of Bingham and Beveridge, the theological influence of George Hickes, and the principles laid down by the committee for the design of the fifty churches; the link is exemplified by Nicholas Hawksmoor's plan for 'The Basilica after the Primitive Christians' of c.1712.[3]

When the commission for building the fifty new churches was formed, the commissioners sought the best advice available on how they should proceed. On the one hand, Wren submitted his letter on the auditory church; on the other, Vanbrugh insisted that the churches 'should not only serve for the accomodation of the inhabitants . . . , but at the same time remain monuments to Posterity of . . . Piety and Grandeur, and by Consequence become Ornaments to the Towne, and a Credit to the Nation.'[146] But a decisive submission was also made by Hickes, who replied to Vanbrugh's advice in 'Observations on Mr. Van Brugg's proposals about Buildinge the new Churches'. Hickes was not a member of the commission; his name never even appears in the minutes. This is hardly surprising, given that he was deprived of the deanery of Worcester as a Nonjuror and was the Nonjuring bishop of Thetford. But the influence of his 'Observations' on both the written plans of the commission and Hawksmoor's architectural plans is clear. Hickes's involvement is further evidence of the continued close identity of juring and nonjuring theology—indeed the churches influenced by the commission's plans might be seen as architectural expressions of the principles of the dynamic receptionist and the virtualist schools of eucharistic theology.

---

[1] Nicolaus Pevsner, *An Outline of European Architecture* (Penguin Books, Harmondsworth, 1943) pp.133–134.

[2] See Howard Colvin, 'Introduction' in E.G.W. Bill, ed. *The Queen Anne Churches. A Catalogue of Papers in the Lambeth Palace Library of the Commission for Building Fifty New Churches in London and Westminster 1711–1759* (Mansell, London, 1979) pp.xi–xii.

[3] Pierre de la Ruffiniere du Prey, 'Hawksmoor's "Basilica after the Primitive Christians": Architecture and Theology', in *Journal of the Society of Architectural Historians* XLVIII:38–52 (March 1989).

[4] *The Queen Anne Churches* p.xi.

At a meeting of 11 July 1712 a committee laid out principles for the design of the churches. Among them were the following:

'5. One general design or form to be agreed upon for all the fifty new intended churches, where sites will admit thereof; the steeples or towers excepted.

8. There be at East end of each church two small rooms, one for vestments, another for vessels or other consecrated things....

10. Fonts in each church be so large as to permit Baptism by dipping when desired.

11. All pews be single and of equal height, so low that every person in them may be seen either kneeling or sitting, and all facing the communion table . . . .

13. Chancel be raised three steps above nave or body of the church.'[147]

Hickes in his 'Observations' called for vestries at the east end of the church 'for keeping the sacerdotal Robes, and holy Vessels'; for a baptistry at the west end with a font 'large and deep enough for immersion'[148]; for an ascent of three steps between nave and chancel; and for the east-west orientation of the churches. The careful provision of vestries (No. 8), the attention given to the font (No. 10), the orientation of the low pews toward the communion table (No. 11), and the raising up of the chancel above the nave (No. 13) all reveal the sacramental bias of the design. On the whole, these instructions envisaged a church on the primitive basilican model, a church which would conform to Vanbrugh's stress on 'the most Solemn & Awfull Appearance both without and within'.[3]

In response to these recommendations of plans Nicholas Hawksmoor produced a proposed design for a site in Bethnal Green which the commissioners in the end did not buy. Tellingly he entitled the design 'The Basilica after the Primitive Christians' with reference to the 'purest times of Christianity' in the fourth century (Ill. 2c). It is a plan clearly in tune with the ecclesiological preoccupations of the time. It is part historical reconstruction, part ideal model, and, as Downes points out, 'each of [its] functions is considered both ecclesiologically and architecturally.'[4] This plan provides in even greater detail for Hickes's recommendations—vestries (D), a 'place for the font for ye Converts which was in ye Porch—& to be immersd' (B), east-west orientation (A), as well as an array of surrounding buildings, all related to Hickes's recommendations.[5]

In the bibliography attached to his 'Observations', Hickes makes clear his debt to 'the third vol. of Mr Bingham's Ecclesiastical Antiquities'. The broad sympathy between Hickes's and Bingham's principles should already be evident, and for details regarding the furnishing and use of primitive churches Hickes and Hawksmoor would naturally have turned to the *Origines Ecclesiasticae* as a compendium of all available evidence on early churches. It is worth noting that Hawksmoor does not use the term 'basilica' in its precise

---

[1] M.H. Port, ed. *The Commissions for Building Fifty New Churches. The Minute Books, 1711-27, A Calendar.* (London, London Record Society) 1986, p.xiv.

[2] The requirement for fonts large enough to accomodate infant baptism by dipping rather than infusion also reflects the influence of the early church, where baptism by immersion was the norm. John Johnson, that enthusiast for all things primitive, went so far as to install in his church at Cranbrook a font large enough for the baptism of adults by immersion in the hope of attracting Baptists into the church. The font remains to this day.

[3] Kerry Downes, *Hawksmoor* (Thames & Hudson, London, 1970) p.105. A helpful article on the background to the fifty churches is R.A. Beddard, 'Ecclesiastical and Liturgical Background' in 'Hawksmoor's Christ Church Spitalfields' *Architectural Design* vol. 49 no. 7 (1979).

[4] Downes, *Hawksmoor* 1970 pp.106–107.

[5] Du Prey, 'Hawksmoor', p.44.

architectural sense of a building with colonnaded aisles and an apse, but rather as a generic term for a church; Bingham had already noted that this was the sense in which the early church used the term.[1] Bingham also provided a variety of plans based on textual evidence which are reflected in the planned and completed churches. For example, the provision of rooms flanking the chancel for vestments and holy vessels (these rooms appear not only in Hawksmoor's "Basilica" but also in his, Thomas Archer's and James Gibbs's churches) corresponds (according to the requirements of Anglican worship) to the *Prothesis* and the *Diaconicum* to be found on either side of the bema as depicted in the *Ichnographiae Templorum Beverigij* and *Jacobi Goar* (Ill. 2).

The 'Primitive Basilica' was never built as such (although St George in the East is closest to it in plan). But all of Hawksmoor's churches were clearly built in its spirit; 'His churches are a perfect extension of the synoptical principles contained in the *Origines Ecclesiasticae*.'[2] The first church to be built under the Act was St Alfege, Greenwich. An engraving of the church after Hawksmoor of 1714 demonstrates the continued influence of the 'Basilica after the Primitive Christians': there is the same generic use of 'basilica', a western *baptisterium*, and eastern vestries flanking the altar. The altar rails are even called *cancelli* after the rails around the altar enclosure in early churches. Inside the small size of the chancel is compensated by an extremely ornate treatment, with illusionist painting of coffers, trophies made with the instruments of the passion (sacrificial emphasis), and carvings by Grinling Gibbons of the capitals and entablatures of the altarpiece, 'which consists of a reredos flanked by Borrominesque groups of columns supporting concave entablatures'[3]. At St Mary Woolnoth twisted Corinthian columns support a ciborium within a proscenium arch (Ill. 4b), while at St Anne Limehouse the altar is given an equally impressive and theatrical setting. Finally, at Christ Church Spitalfields, Hawksmoor developed 'the design ... from a longitudinal columnar church, nearer the strict form of a basilica than was the "Primitive Christian" plan ...'[4] Here several elements highlight the importance of the eucharist, including the Palladian window over the reredos and the magnificent chancel beam on Corinthian columns striding across the entrance to the chancel like a triumphal gateway.[5]

James Gibbs, a Roman Catholic, was also an early architect to the commission although he built only one church for it, St Mary-le-Strand. Here too a triumphal archway leads the way into the heavenly places of the deep chancel with its semi-circular apse in the basilican tradition.[6] The chancel ceiling is extravagantly decorated with the full range of

---

[1] Du Prey locates in Bingham the sources for many of Hickes's recommendations: *op. cit.* p.46.

[2] Du Prey, 'Hawksmoor', p.47.

[3] Downes, *Hawksmoor* 1979, pp.170.

[4] Downes, *Hawksmoor* 1970, pp.157–158.

[5] It is interesting to note that Hawksmoor anticipated Comper's 'unity by inclusion', the essential elements of which included a gothic screen and a classical ciborium (Comper, *Atmosphere* pp.21–22). At Beverley Minster Hawksmoor 'supervised repairs and embellishments ... including the addition of a "Gothick" choir screen, nave galleries on Doric pillars, and a Corinthian baldacchino (all since destroyed).'Downes, *Hawksmoor* 1970, p.160.

[6] The use of the apse was not confined to such large and rich churches. Several small plain brick churches on the Eastern Shore of Maryland have small apses in which their altars are placed, e.g. Old Trinity, Church Creek (1674) and St Luke's, Church Hill (1731). The external sign of the function of the church is again significant here.

symbolic iconography: cherub's heads, the tetragrammaton in a glory, a dove descending, bunches of grapes and ears of wheat, all in a flamboyant Roman baroque style. As Gibbs himself noted of the chancel, 'The Commissioners . . . spar'd no cost to beautify it'[1] (Ill. 4a). Terry Friedman suggests that St Mary's blatantly Roman associations were a basic cause of Gibbs's dismissal from the commission; this is unlikely, since we have already seen all these elements from blamelessly 'Protestant' hands. More likely is that Gibbs's own Roman Catholicism and likely Jacobitism were unacceptable to the resurgent Whigs in power.[2]

Although Gibbs lost his job with the commission, he continued to be employed as architect of Anglican churches in which he continued to employ the principles laid down in 1712. Among the most notable of these churches were St Peter's Vere Street (the Marylebone Chapel, 1724) and particularly St Martin-in-the-Fields (1726). Gibbs chose the form he did at St Martin's because it was most 'capacious and convenient' to accommodate a large congregation able to view the communion table and pulpit with equal ease. As planned there was ample space for communicants in front of the rails; the chancel is raised three steps above the nave and is flanked by vestry rooms. The design of St Martin's has been particularly important—Gavin Stamp has called it 'one of the most influential and imitated buildings in architectural history'.[3] St Martin's and the Marylebone Chapel would become models for such North American churches as Peter Harrison's King's Chapel, Boston, and Christ Church, Cambridge; St Paul's, Halifax; St Peter's, Philadelphia; St Paul's Chapel, New York; St Philip's and St Michael's, Charleston; and the Anglican Cathedral of the Holy Trinity, Quebec City.[4] Through Gibbs's influence, the design of the Anglican 'primitive basilica' was disseminated throughout the English-speaking world.

[1] James Gibbs, *A Book of Architecture, containing Designs of Buildings and Ornaments* (London, 1728) p.vi. See pl. 16 for the decoration of the ceiling and apse. I am indebted to Peter Maplestone, churchwarden of St Mary's, for showing me the relevant chapter of his forthcoming history of the church.
[2] Terry Friedman, *James Gibbs* (Yale University Press, New Haven, 1984) pp.48–51.
[3] Gavin Stamp, 'Church Architecture' in Robert Fermor-Hesketh, ed. *Architecture of the British Empire* (Weidenfeld and Nicolson, London, 1986) p.149.
[4] Friedman, *James Gibbs* pp.277–280.

Ill. 4a
Ceiling of apse, St. Mary-le Strand,
James Gibbs (1714-19

Ill. 4b
Ciborium and altar,
St. Mary Woolnoth
Nicholas Hawksmoor (1716-24)

Ill. 4c
St. Katherine, Chiselhampton, Oxon. (1762)

4. Conclusion

What then are we to make of this mass of information and what does it say about how we should treat our churches, those of the eighteenth as well as other centuries? I believe it means that architectural reordering may not be necessary to worship in the spirit of the modern liturgical movement; the congregation might consider reordering itself during the service rather than altering the building. This principle is as applicable to traditional nave and chancel churches as to auditory churches. If the liturgical movement has really been about reappropriating the spirit of worship of the early church, then the eighteenth century has much to teach us. There is no reason a contemporary liturgy cannot be appropriately celebrated in a church like Chiselhampton (Ill. 4c). Box pews were not built so high to obscure the altar; when people were in them, they were looking at the priest and clerk higher up in the reading desk and pulpit. When the eucharist was celebrated the people left the pews and went to the altar. Congregations should not be afraid of movement—they need not stay stuck in one place. What a wonderful symbol it would be if the people came out their individual pews at the peace to greet one another and go together up to the altar for the eucharist. In the dynamic sense of direction to be found in these eighteenth-century churches, from font to Word to altar and beyond towards the eschaton, we may also have much to learn. The westward celebration does have the advantage of emphasizing the communal meal aspect of the eucharist, but it may also encourage a sense of closure and self-sufficiency. When the intention is to emphasize the common eucharistic prayer of priest and people, the focus on the priest behind the table may tend to suggest the dissonant notion of the priest as the *icon Christi*, a substitution of clerical for corporate worship. We need to recover the early church's focus on the eschatological thrust of the eucharist, a being open to the world and to our future in Christ that is summarized in the proclamation 'Christ has died; Christ is risen; Christ will come again.' The congregation gathering close with its priest before the altar would negate any sense of division between celebrant and people. Our present goal ought not to be 'making the building serve the liturgy' in the sense of chopping and changing our churches to serve the current fashion. Eighteenth-century churches have already been built to serve the liturgy. Even many traditional gothic nave and chancel churches could easily accommodate a congregation moving from the ministry of the word in the nave to the eschatological feast in the chancel. Would it not be preferable to use the worship space creatively in this way rather than subjecting the churches to drastic reorderings that deprive them of their intended architectural unity and integrity? We owe it to our churches and to our departed fellow-worshippers who built them to be sensitive enough to discover their original vision of worship and so creatively to adapt it for ourselves that we might more truly worship with the whole communion of saints, past, present, and future.

THE GROUP FOR RENEWAL OF WORSHIP (GROW)

This group, originally founded in 1961, has for over twenty-five years taken responsibility for the Grove Books publications on liturgy and worship. Its membership and broad aims reflect a highly reforming, pastoral and missionary interest in worship. Beginning with a youthful evangelical Anglican membership in the early 1970s, the Group has not only probed adventurously into the future of Anglican worship, but has also with growing sureness of touch taken its place in promoting weighty scholarship. Thus the list of 'Grove Liturgical Studies' shows how, over a twelve-year period, the quarterly Studies added steadily to the material available to students of patristic, reformation and modern scholarly issues in liturgy. In 1986 the Group was approached by the Alcuin Club Committee with a view to publishing the new series of Joint Liturgical Studies, and this series is, at the time of writing, in its eleventh year of publication, sustaining the programme with three Studies each year.

Between the old Grove Liturgical Studies and the new Joint Liturgical Studies there is a large provision of both English language texts and other theological works on the patristic era. A detailed consolidated list is available from the publishers.

Since the early 1970s the Group has had Colin Buchanan as chairman and Trevor Lloyd as vice-chairman.

THE ALCUIN CLUB

The Alcuin Club exists to promote the study of Christian liturgy in general, and in particular the liturgies of the Anglican Communion. Since its foundation in 1897 it has published over 130 books and pamphlets. Members of the Club receive some publications of the current year free and others at a reduced rate.

Information concerning the annual subscription, applications for membership and lists of publications is obtainable from the Treasurer, The Revd. T. R. Barker, 11 Abbey Street, Chester CH1 2JE (Tel. 01244 347811, Fax. 01244 347823).

The Alcuin Club has a three-year arrangement with the Liturgical Press, Collegeville, whereby the old tradition of an annual Alcuin Club major scholarly study has been restored. The first title under this arrangement was published in early 1993: Alastair McGregor, *Fire and Light: The Symbolism of Fire and Light in the Holy Week Services.* The second was Martin Dudley, *The Collect in Anglican Liturgy;* the third is Gordon Jeanes, *The Day has Come! Easter and Baptism in Zeno of Verona.*

The Joint Liturgical Studies have been reduced to three per annum from 1992, and the Alcuin Club subscription now includes the annual publication (as above) and the three Joint Liturgical Studies (with an extra in 1994). The full list of Joint Liturgical Studies is printed overleaf. All titles but no. 4 are in print.

Alcuin/GROW Joint Liturgical Studies

All cost £3.95 (US $8) in 1997

1987 TITLES

1. **(LS 49) Daily and Weekly Worship—from Jewish to Christian**
   by Roger Beckwith, Warden of Latimer House, Oxford
2. **(LS 50) The Canons of Hippolytus** edited by Paul Bradshaw, Professor of Liturgics, University of Notre Dame.
3. **(LS 51) Modern Anglican Ordination Rites** edited by Colin Buchanan, then Bishop of Aston
4. **(LS 52) Models of Liturgical Theology** by James Empereur, of the Jesuit School of Theology, Berkeley

1988 TITLES

5. **(LS 53) A Kingdom of Priests: Liturgical Formation of the Laity: The Brixen Essays**
   edited by Thomas Talley, Professor of Liturgics, General Theological Seminary, New York
6. **(LS 54) The Bishop in Liturgy: an Anglican Study** edited by Colin Buchanan, then Bishop of Aston
7. **(LS 55) Inculturation: the Eucharist in Africa** by Phillip Tovey
8. **(LS 56) Essays in Early Eastern Initiation** edited by Paul Bradshaw,

1989 TITLES

9. **(LS 57) The Liturgy of the Church in Jerusalem** by John Baldovin
10. **(LS 58) Adult Initiation** edited by Donald Withey
11. **(LS 59) 'The Missing Oblation': The Contents of the earlyAntiochene Anaphota** by John Fenwick
12. **(LS 60) Calvin and Bullinger on the Lord's Supper** by Paul Rorem

1990 TITLES

13-14 **(LS 61) The Liturgical Portions of the Apostolic Constitutions: A Text for Students**
   edited by W. Jardine Grisbrooke (This double-size volume costs double price (i.e. £7.90 in 1997))
15 **(LS 62) Liturgical Inculturation in the Anglican Communion** edited by David Holeton
16. **(LS 63) Cremation Today and Tomorrow** by Douglas Davies, University of Nottingham

1991 TITLES

17. **(LS 64) The Preaching Service—The Glory of the Methodists**
   by Adrian Burdon, Methodist Minister in Rochdale
18. **(LS 65) Irenaeus of Lyon on Baptism and Eucharist**
   edited with Introduction, Translation and Commentary by David Power, Washington D.C.
19. **(LS 66) Testamentum Domini** edited by Grant Sperry-White, Department of Theology, Notre Dame
20. **(LS 67) The Origins of the Roman Rite** Edited by Gordon Jeanes, then Lecturer in Liturgy, University of Durham

1992 TITLES

21. **The Anglican Eucharist in New Zealand 1814-1989** by Bosco Peters, Christchurch, New Zealand
22-23 **Foundations of Christian Music: The Music of Pre-Constantinian Christianity**
   by Edward Foley, Capuchin Franciscan, Chicago (second double-sized volume at £7.90 in 1997)

1993 TITLES

24. **Liturgical Presidency** by Paul James
25. **The Sacramentary of Sarapion of Thmuis: A Text for Students**
   edited by Ric Lennard-Barrett, West Australia
26. **Communion Outside the Eucharist** by Phillip Tovey, Banbury, Oxon

1994 TITLES

27. **Revising the Eucharist: Groundwork for the Anglican Communion** edited by David Holeton
28. **Anglican Liturgical Inculturation in Africa** edited by David Gitari, Bishop of Kirinyaga, Kenya
29-30. **On Baptismal Fonts: Ancient and Modern**
   by Anita Stauffer, Lutheran World Federation, Geneva (Double-sized volume at £7.90)

1995 TITLES

31. **The Comparative Liturgy of Anton Baumstark** by Fritz West
32. **Worship and Evangelism in Pre-Christendom** by Alan Kreider
33. **Liturgy in Early Christian Egypt** by Maxwell E. Johnson

1996 TITLES

34. **Welcoming the Baptized** by Timothy Turner
35. **Daily Prayer in the Reformed Tradition: An Initial Survey** by Diane Karay Tripp
36. **The Ritual Kiss in Early Christian Worship** by Edward Phillips

1997 TITLES

37. **'After the Primitive Christians': The Eighteenth-century Anglican Eucharist in its Architectural Set**
   ting by Peter Doll
38. **Coronations Past, Present and Future** edited by Paul Bradshaw (September, 1997)
39. [To be announced]

Grove Liturgical Studies

This series began in March 1975, and was published quarterly until 1986. Each title has 32 or 40 pages. No's 1, 3-6, 9, 10, 16, 36, 44 and 46 are out of print. Asterisked numbers have been reprinted. Prices in 1997. £2.75.